D1172878

THE MANAGER'S GUIDE TO DISTRIBUTION CHANNELS

THE MANAGER'S GUIDE TO DISTRIBUTION CHANNELS

Linda Gorchels
Edward J. Marien
Chuck West

McGraw-Hill

New York Chicago San Francisco Lisbon
London Madrid Mexico City Milan New Delhi
San Juan Seoul Singapore Sydney Toronto

The **McGraw·Hill** *Companies*

1 2 3 4 5 6 7 8 9 0 DOC/DOC 0 9 8 7 6 5 4

ISBN 0-07-142868-2

This publication is designed to provide accurate and authoritative information in regard to the subject matter covered. It is sold with the understanding that neither the author nor the publisher is engaged in rendering legal, accounting, or other professional service. If legal advice or other expert assistance is required, the services of a competent professional person should be sought.

—From a Declaration of Principles jointly adopted by a Committee of the American Bar Association and a Committee of Publishers

McGraw-Hill books are available at special quantity discounts to use as premiums and sales promotions, or for use in corporate training programs. For more information, please write to the Director of Special Sales, McGraw-Hill, 2 Penn Plaza, New York, NY 10121-2298. Or contact your local bookstore.

Library of Congress Cataloging-in-Publication Data
Gorchels, Linda.
  The manager's guide to distribution channels / by Linda Gorchels, Chuck West, Edward Marien.
      p. cm.
  ISBN 0-07-142868-2 (hardcover : alk. paper)
  1. Marketing channels. I. West, Chuck. II. Marien, Edward J. III. Title.
HF5415.129.G67 2004
658.8'7--dc22

                                                                2003026032

CONTENTS

Preface   ix

Part One. An Executive Overview of Channel Structure   **1**

1. **Understanding Distribution**   **3**
   Strategic Fit   3
   Management Issues   14
   Stages of Channel Redesign   20
   Key Points   21

2. **Forces Shaping Channel Strategy**   **23**
   Channel Strategy as Part of Overall Business Strategy   23
   External Forces Impacting Channel Strategy   28
   Internal Forces Shaping Channel Strategy   36
   Key Points   44

3. **Supply Chain Management**   **45**
   Fulfilling the Demands of Supply Chain Trading Partners   45
   Supply Chain Core Processes   52
   Key Points   53

4. **Legal Issues and the Reseller Contract**   **55**
   Terminology   56
   The Legal Side of Marketing Policies   57
   Written Contracts   61
   Key Points   66

Part Two. Strategic Decisions   **67**

5. Clarifying Requirements:
   A Roadmap for Business Executives   **69**
   Define Channel and Coverage Requirements   69
   Develop Channel Design   81
   Select Suitable Channel Partners   83
   Establish Mutual Performance Expectations   83
   Improve Channel Effectiveness   84
   Monitor Performance and Adjust Plans   85
   Key Points   87

6. Channel Design   **90**
   Revisiting Channel Goals   91
   Renovating Existing Channels   94
   Managing Multiple Channels   97
   Building Hybrid Channels   100
   Key Points   104

7. International Channel Design   **105**
   Targeting World Markets   105
   Evaluating Different International Channel Structures   107
   Selecting the Right Channel Partners   109
   Managing the Channel   115
   Key Points   116

8. Selecting Suitable Channel Partners   **118**
   Search Methodology   119
   Assessing Your Channel Candidate   123
   Recruit and Sign the Best Candidates   125
   Key Points   129

Part Three. Managing the Ongoing Relationship   **131**

9. Understanding the Distributor's World:
   Implications for Suppliers   **133**
   Distributor Definitions   133
   Manufacturer's Influence   134
   Forces of Change   135
   Manufacturing and Distributor Differences   138
   Changes in Distributor Operations   141
   Changes in Manufacturer and Distributor Relationships   142
   Strategic Implications for Manufacturers   143
   Key Points   146

10. Establishing Mutual Performance Expectations   **147**
  Traditional Role Expectations   147
  Manufacturer Plans   149
  Distributor Plans   151
  Distributor Profiles   155
  How Distributors Evaluate Manufacturers   158
  Penetration Index   159
  Key Points   160

11. Improving Channel Effectiveness   **161**
  Six Components to Improve Channel Effectiveness   161
  Selling to Your Distributors   163
  Selecting a Product Champion or Product-Line Specialist   166
  Coaching Your Product-Line Specialist   168
  Distributor Sales Training   182
  Using Promotions and Advertising   188
  Acting as a Business Consultant   193
  Key Points   194

12. Monitoring Performance and Adjusting Plans   **195**
  Performance Monitoring   195
  Adjustments   208
  Key Points   210

  Index   **213**

PREFACE

Congratulations on your first step in improving your distribution channel strategy. By reading *The Manager's Guide to Distribution Channels,* you'll uncover a framework to develop, implement, evaluate, and benchmark channel strategy. Combining our experiences and perspectives from a variety of industries, we provide you with a book that goes beyond a review of theories and concepts to a process generating *real* ideas that you as a manager can use today.

Manage in an Environment of Change

Companies have found that even with a superior product, strong marketing communications, and a fair price, market share can drop when there is insufficient attention provided to channel strategy. This book equips managers with a practical understanding of both channel and supply chain management principles to help them be more productive in contemporary channel situations. The splintering of channels, the impact of technology, and the balancing of large channel partners with traditional smaller and regional operations are just some of the factors escalating the rate of change in the channel environment.

A critical theme throughout the book is the importance of end-user needs, wants, and satisfaction in the design of a "go to market" strategy. By working backwards from the end customer and the requirements for your products and services to be effectively sold, a blueprint of an appropriate channel design emerges. Following this blueprint with a set of tools for managing and monitoring ongoing performance leads to strong business development results.

High Impact Tools

The book is designed not just to be *read*, but also to be *used*. You'll find different approaches to:

- Segmenting your channel
- Renovating existing channels, managing multiple channels, and building hybrid channels
- Selecting suitable channel partners
- Selling methods for moving your product *into* and *through* the distribution channels

There are numerous templates, checklists, and worksheets supplied throughout the book including:

- An example distributor satisfaction survey (chapter 5)
- A template for assessing distributor or channel candidates (chapter 8)
- A distributor business plan outline (chapter 10)
- A template outlining a cooperative advertising program (chapter 11)
- An in-depth performance review worksheet (chapter 12)

You'll also find advice on establishing effective product champions within your distributors and improving training programs for your channel.

A Practical Framework

The book guides readers through the steps required to strategically and tactically manage channels to increase performance. It provides a practical yet rigorous understanding of what channels are, how they work, how they are used, and how to make them more effective for your organization.

Part One provides an overview of channel structure, with the intent of providing you with "strategic intuition" on how to successfully link business strategy with channel execution. It introduces the seven stages of channel redesign that become the focus of the remainder of the book.

Part Two helps executives make the strategic decisions related to establishing the blueprint for channel strategy, including defining channel and coverage requirements, developing channel design, and selecting suitable channel partners.

Part Three provides powerful tools that executives can use to focus their attention and resources on the day-to-day management of ongoing channel relationships.

Intended Audience

The book is designed for managers and executives who want to improve channel effectiveness and efficiency for getting their products and services to their end-customers. Anyone involved in making decisions about distribution strategy, or in implementing those decisions, can benefit from the concrete systems framework presented.

Acknowledgments

This book would not have been possible without the atmosphere provided by the executive education department of the UW-Madison School of Business, where all three authors are faculty members. We would especially like to thank the following people who broadened our perspectives and helped us develop and refine the ideas and tools presented in the book:

- ▶ Our employers prior to the university for the experiences and training we obtained in on-the-job situations.
- ▶ The executive participants of our professional development workshops for openly sharing their ideas from the wide variety of industries they represent.
- ▶ Our consulting clients for giving us an insider's look into their challenges and opportunities.

Without question, their combined input substantially enhanced the book.

In addition, we would like to express our personal thanks to:

▶ Our editor, Catherine Dassopoulos from McGraw-Hill, and our compositor John Woods and the team at CWL Publishing Enterprises.

▶ Our spouses (Chuck Gorchels, Cindy West, and Janet Marien) for their encouragement and support, and "picking up the slack" during this project.

Part One
An Executive Overview of Channel Structure

Chapter 1

UNDERSTANDING DISTRIBUTION

For products or services to be successful in the marketplace, they must be a where and a how for customers who want to buy them. In addition, what support, processes, or environment (tangibles) are necessary to help would-be customers make buying decisions? Is a showroom required for customers to view and "try out" a product? How important is immediate fulfillment from inventory? What channels are consistent with the way customers want to buy? Is your firm effective (or even present) in those channels?

Banks have opened branches in grocery stores and now provide phone and Internet account accessibility. Some industrial firms have augmented their traditional channels with "big box" retailers to either reach new customers or offer existing customers more options. These changes are prompting companies to examine distribution strategies and make either strategic or tactical changes or both. The continuum of distribution issues is shown in Figure 1-1.

Strategic Fit

Dell Inc. is a company that has long focused on a direct channel to reach its customers, being a leader in direct sales by telephone and the Internet. Later, it added kiosks in shopping malls as another way

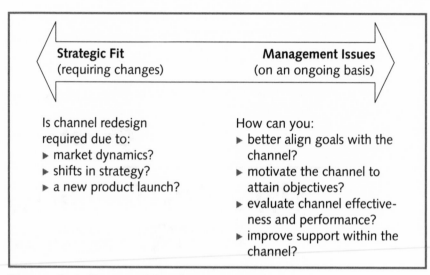

Figure 1-1. Range of distribution issues

to reach consumers. Next, the growth of "white-box PCs" (no-name computers put together from parts of various suppliers) to small businesses through dealers spurred Dell to evaluate this channel as well. Because many small businesses essentially view local dealers as their information technology (IT) department, they are less inclined to purchase direct. They value the training, installation, and repair services they get from the dealer, as well as the face-to-face contact. To reach this group of customers, Dell began offering an unbranded PC to U.S. dealers.[1]

Many other firms have made strategic channel changes. Avon decided to augment its direct consumer sales channel because the average age of the customers of its traditional channel was slowly increasing. The company decided to open boutiques in JC Penney stores to reach a younger, working market. Avon's new retail line is tar-

Are the end customers the starting point for my channel decisions?
- ▶ Have I given thought to how the end customers want to buy my products?
- ▶ Does my existing channel provide the attributes they want?
- ▶ What am I doing or not doing today that could be changed to make tomorrow better?

geting women ages 25 to 29; its typical customer ranges in age from 40 to 55.[2] Similarly, many industrial companies have augmented their traditional direct or distributor sales channels with Internet ordering for specific products or customers.

A channel is commonly defined as a "set of interdependent organizations involved in the process of making a product or service available for consumption or use."[3] This process can include the physical movement, warehousing, and/or ownership of the product; presale, transaction, and postsale activities; order processing, credit, and collections; and various support services. Marketing channels are also defined as "vertical value-adding chains that create competitive advantage."[4]

A firm may use a variety of direct sales channels—a direct sales force, telesales, direct mail, the Internet, and company-owned stores—and indirect sales channels—independent reps, distributors, dealers, and retailers. Manufacturers' or independent reps are individuals or agencies that function as an external sales force for a firm. Sometimes called brokers or agents, these organizations bring together the buyer and seller, generally do not take title, and are paid through commissions. Most industrial reps carry noncompeting products from many firms, but this is not as true for consumer reps.

Distributors and wholesalers generally buy products, are compensated through discounts off list price, and usually sell to customers out of inventory; the customers could be other resellers, integrators, manufacturers, or the end users. Special types of distributors include value-added resellers (VARs) and dealers. Definitions of some common terms related to distribution channels are included in the box just below. It's worth noting that the distinction between types of intermediaries is blurring, and many manufacturers are creating *hybrid* channels by contracting to have necessary functions performed by businesses that may or may not have been part of the traditional channel.

Big box reseller	An intermediary focused more on moving volume than providing specialized services. Examples include Wal-Mart and Home Depot.
Broker	Independent sales force (generally for consumer products) that negotiates contracts of purchase and sale.

	Examples include the food, apparel, and health-care industries.
Buying group	Loose affiliate of companies that buys in quantity from a distributor or manufacturer, mostly to gain volume discounts. Some may be cooperatives.
Catalog house	A company that buys and stocks a line of products, sold through printed or electronic catalogs.
Channel	A group of independent and interdependent organizations involved in the sale and movement of goods and services to the end users. May be called a distribution, marketing, or sales channel or network.
Dealer	An independent reseller, generally authorized by one or a limited number of vendors to provide support to end users. Examples include heavy equipment dealers and auto dealers.
Export management company	An international form of broker or independent sales agency.
Franchisee	A company given the right or license to market a firm's goods or services in a given territory, often with special trademark or brand privileges, as well as franchise fees. Examples include fast food outlets.
General line distributor	A company that purchases, stocks, and resells a wide range of products to end users or resellers.
Hybrid channel	A nontraditional channel created by piecing together functions (such as sales, fulfillment, installation, repair, etc.) performed by companies specializing in that activity. May also be called a synthetic channel. For example, a plumbing company may have leads generated at Home Depot, with installation and servicing handled by contractor dealers.
Independent rep/agent	A company that provides sales expertise to give a manufacturer local market coverage, generally without taking title to or carrying inventory of a product. May also be called a manufacturer's rep or agent, sales rep, broker, or agency. Consumer reps frequently represent competing products, whereas industrial reps are more apt to handle complementary products.

Influencers/ specifiers	Firms or individuals that influence the flow of products by how an opportunity is specified. Examples include architects, designers, consultants.
Integrators	Businesses that provide consulting services, total systems, and implementation services for end customers.
Jobber	A limited service wholesaler providing services such as delivery, shelving, inventory carrying, and financing.
Master distributor	A distributor that buys in sufficient quantity to supply to smaller resellers and dealers.
MRO distributor	A distributor that carries maintenance, repair and operating supplies. A synonymous term for MRO is facilities maintenance supplies. An example is W.W. Grainger.
Outsourcing	Process of contracting with companies to provide services in an area in which they have particular expertise (e.g., a manufacturer contracting with a distributor to manage a repair part stockroom for the manufacturer).
Physical distribution	The product flow to customers through a defined network of transportation links and storage. Also referred to as logistics.
Reseller/ intermediary	A company that buys and resells a product.
Specialty distributor	A reseller that offers specialized services, such as engineering support, as well as buying, stocking, and reselling products.
Stocking reseller	A company that carries inventory. Most distributors and some independent reps carry inventory, but some distributors are nonstocking distributors.
Supply chain	Network from the supplier of raw materials, through manufacturers, warehouses, and resellers, to the end user.
System integrator	A type of VAR that provides technical expertise on complicated, systems-oriented, or solutions-oriented products.
Value-added reseller (VAR)	Reseller that bundles products and services to provide a "one-stop shop" for end customers.
Value chain	All of the major activities a firm and its trading partners perform (e.g., procurement, operations, logistics, etc.) to provide competitive value to customers.

Vertical integration	The decision by a firm to perform the activities of a channel (generally through acquisition of another firm) rather than using the services of independent companies in a channel.
Wholesaler	Distributor who sells into the consumer marketplace.

Channel redesign or refinement may be required to respond to changes in market dynamics, a shift in strategy or a new product launch, as shown in Figure 1-2.

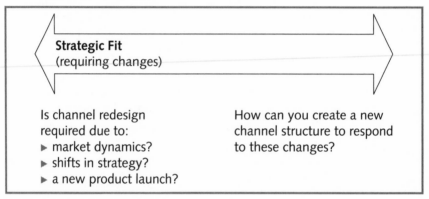

Figure 1-2. Strategic fit issues

Market Dynamics

The growth of the Internet has arguably had a more pronounced impact on channel functioning than almost any other recent external issue. Although the concept of *disintermediation* (i.e., bypassing channel intermediaries through exclusive use of the Internet) has been largely discredited, there is no question that the Internet will continue to play a significant role in channel (or supply chain) operations. Wholesale drop shipping has been used for years by traditional catalog retailers but has grown with the increase in online purchases. Ingram Micro, a computer distributor for companies such as IBM, HP, and Toshiba, has historically drop-shipped products for retailers who called in their orders. However, their drop shipments increased from 70 percent of U.S. orders before e-commerce to 84 percent in 2003.[5]

For manufacturers reaching the consumer market through mass retail channels, the Internet is streamlining ordering and inventory management processes. For example, Wal-Mart Stores, Inc. announced it will require its 10,000 or so midsize suppliers to connect to it through the Internet using a specific set of communication protocols (electronic data interchange or EDI) called EDI-INT AS2.[6] Radio frequency identification (RFID) tags are also a data capture technology that is beginning to impact channel productivity. Point-of-sale (POS) and point-of-installation (POI) technologies are providing important data with which to manage new product introductions and inventory levels as well as to capture results of sales promotions. Wal-Mart has given its major suppliers the requirement to implement RFID tags by 2005. These types of technologies are changing the relationship between manufacturer and reseller, as well as the role of the salesperson responsible for the relationship.

In other situations, consumers are using the Internet to gather information before making significant purchases such as cars; manufacturers will need to work with the channel to provide the best information and sales training or support given the increasingly sophisticated end-consumers.

The Internet has also had an impact on business-to-business (B2B) channels. Some manufacturers are providing e-commerce tools for dealers to incorporate into their Web sites. Honeywell, for example, offers its HVACR (heating, ventilating, air conditioning, and refrigeration) dealers E-StorePro, a customized Web site to help them sell replacement parts and services to contractors. The Web site features unique home pages for contractors, a current Honeywell catalog, and the ability to sell replacement parts and services online.[7] It's become more common for the Internet to be used as a tool to *enhance* the relationship between reseller and end user because a major asset of a B2B channel is the quality of relationships with end customers.

In addition to technology, regulatory changes might prompt a company or an industry to rethink the traditional marketing channels. The Gramm-Leach-Bliley Act of 1999, for example, repealed former restrictions on financial institutions and facilitates affiliations among banks, securities firms, and insurance companies. New channels have emerged as a result of this regulation. Nationwide Financial Services has targeted certified public accounts as a new distribution channel for its retirement and other financial services.[8] Insurance companies are selling their products through banks, causing the percentage of life insurance policies sold through captive insurance agents to decline.[9]

Industrial distribution is experiencing major changes with the momentum shifting in the direction of consolidation. Some economists predict that many of the major fields will be dominated by a select number of top distributors and that industrial buyers will reduce the number of distributors they deal with. Integrated supply, contract selling, and reverse auctions will impact the concept of value-added selling.[10] These changes are triggering shifts in corporate strategies—and consequently shifts in channel strategies—for a number of organizations.

Strategy Shifts

In a perfect world, manufacturers would select distributors on the basis of strategic compatibility. However, the compatibility may be affected by external factors (as mentioned in the last section) or by internal factors such as mergers and acquisitions or expansions into new markets or industries.

Companies engage in mergers and acquisitions to gain access to new markets, manufacturing or operating competencies, or other means of improving their competitive advantage. Sears acquired Lands' End in 2002, for example, to gain a fashion line of clothing and experience in direct marketing; at the same time Lands' End gained additional market access through the Sears outlets.

In most cases, however, there is generally little thought given to the relative "fit" of the acquired channels. In reevaluating channel strategy, it is necessary to determine

1. the expectations of the various customer segments,
2. the approaches used by competition to reach customers,
3. the skill sets and contract terms of both new and old intermediaries, and
4. the selling requirements of the product lines.

As shown in the Dell example presented earlier, many small businesses (especially those without an internal IT department) may prefer to buy computers from a business that not only supplies the product but also provides the related services. A significant percentage of these customers would not find a direct channel satisfactory. How satisfied are your customers with your existing channel(s)? Ask yourself the following questions:

▶ Do your target customers like to purchase a "bundle" of products (perhaps even from competitors) with one invoice?
▶ Do they want 24/7 ordering capabilities?
▶ Do they want to test the product or see it demonstrated?
▶ Do they want a product customized to their unique needs?

While developing a "go to market" strategy that addresses customer preferences, it's also important to determine what can be done to maintain a competitive advantage. If an indirect channel best satisfies customer needs, for example, chances are high that competitors will also be present in the channel. Therefore, your success will depend partly on your ability to motivate channel members to implement the marketing plan for your product.

Sometimes your best chance at maintaining a competitive advantage is through a hybrid channel. Gateway's channel, for example, is a cross between the direct approach used by Dell and the indirect mass retail channels of Hewlett-Packard. The Gateway approach allows customers to create a custom computer while giving them chances to see tangible products and have face-to-face discussions with a salesperson.

Volvo GM Heavy Truck Corporation also created a hybrid channel. It found that although dealers could predict scheduled maintenance demand quite well, they were not as effective in estimating demand for emergency roadside service. Therefore, Volvo set up a warehouse in Memphis to stock the full line of truck parts and contracted with FedEx to handle the necessary shipments.[11] In both of these examples, channel design changes were made by examining the desired *functions*, and then determining the best way to provide those functions, even if the process required going beyond the "traditional" channel structure.

In some cases, competitive advantage comes from selecting the right type of intermediary—one that provides the most appropriate services for the target customer. If you think in terms of "buying distribution services" rather than "selling through a distribution channel," your focus will shift to the types of services (or functions) most appropriate for addressing needs of the end customer. If customers want to see a tangible product, a channel with a showroom may be necessary. If customers want to be able to immediately and conveniently buy a product and take it with them, a channel with numerous locations may be required. If customers want to have a product delivered and installed, a channel offering those services is critical.

Once the requirements for the channel(s) are determined, it is important to determine how to most profitably meet them. Which services can (should) your firm provide, and which ones can (should) intermediaries provide? Even when you determine that the most *cost-effective* route is to pay a channel (e.g., distributors) to provide the services, your firm must monitor the quality of services to avoid damage to brand equity. Remember that *cost-effective* does not always equate to long-term profitability.

Whenever a company has more than one path to the market, potential exists for channel conflict. Some resellers may resent other channels that offer a lower price point to the same customer. Therefore, companies try to reduce the potential for conflict through various strategies. One approach is to segregate the channels by customer types; for example, one channel may focus on hospitals, while another may focus on industrial firms.

Another approach, where the conflict may be between direct and independent sales forces, may be to designate certain customers as key accounts to be handled exclusively by the company sales force, or if follow-up work is necessary from the channel, to compensate the channel appropriately.

New Product Launch

New product launches sometimes require shifts in channel strategy. The type of intermediary—or even a specific channel partner—may impact the new brand positively or negatively. The ability of the channel to provide technical support, customer service, or a particular brand "halo" should be considered.

When Nike brings out new shoes, it generally sells them through outlets such as Niketown to maintain a more contemporary fashion image. But older Nike styles are sold through the mass discount channels.

Huffy discovered the danger of an improper channel fit when it introduced its new Cross Sport bike in the 1990s.

The successful $700 million bike maker did careful research before it launched the Cross Sport, a combination of the sturdy mountain bike popular with teenagers and a thin-framed, nimbler, racing bike.

Huffy conducted two separate series of market focus groups in shopping malls across the country where randomly selected children and adults viewed the bikes and ranked them. The bikes met with shoppers' approval. So far, so good. In the summer of 1991, Cross Sports were shipped out to mass retailers, such as the Kmart and Toys 'R' Us chains where Huffy did most of its business.

But that move was the mistake. As Richard L. Molen, Huffy president and chief executive explains, the researchers missed one key piece of information. These special, hybrid bikes, aimed at adults and (at $159) priced 15 percent higher than other Huffy bikes, needed individual attention by the sort of knowledgeable salespeople who work only in bike specialty shops.

Expecting Huffy's Cross Sports to be sold by the harried general salespeople at the mass retailers was "a $5 million mistake," says Molen. By 1992, the company had slashed Cross Sport production 7 percent and recorded an earnings drop of 30 percent.[12]

Other Considerations

There may be other brand questions a channel manager should consider. How will your channel partners be identified? Will you provide them with a graphic mark that indicates their affiliation with your company? Are there specific requirements to earn the right to use this mark? Do your partners benefit from using your brand? Do you benefit from a co-branding relationship? How will channel activities and requirements change through the product life cycle?

Even without strategic changes such as acquisitions or new product launches, channel requirements may change as a product moves through the life cycle. New-to-the-world products, when launched, may require more selling upfront than later in the life cycle, and staying with the initial channel strategy may be inappropriate.

A study sponsored by *Sales & Marketing Management Magazine* found that more than 60 percent of responding companies switched channels for a product based on its life-cycle requirements.[13] And because most companies have products at different stages in their life cycle, multichannel strategies are frequently necessary.

Companies may use specialized channels to reach new, smaller, or niche markets then turn to broad-based channels to reach large or mature markets. The specialized channels provide value-added functions such as technical, scientific, or engineering expertise (as is the case with a direct channel or with specialized manufacturer's reps); product specialists; or a showroom (as is the case with VARs or specialty distributors).

These types of channels play an important role in introducing new products or supporting select customers. As products become more commodity-like, requiring less demonstration or technical support, broad-based channels such as catalog houses or big-box retailers are appropriate. These channels provide immediate availability of products with few supporting services.

Reflection Point

What distribution changes are necessary to reflect strategic shifts?

▶ Am I using the Internet and other technology to enhance my relationship with both the channel and end customers?

▶ Do I routinely examine channel fit when exploring strategy initiatives?

▶ Does my existing channel provide a competitive advantage or overcome a competitive disadvantage? If not, can functions or services be shifted or augmented to provide advantage?

▶ Is the appropriateness of the channel structure considered when launching new products?

Management Issues

After the right channel structure is in place, continued sales efforts must be supported, and many other important issues need to be addressed on an ongoing basis.

Many companies don't know what their resellers need or what type of support to provide. The first step to improve the relationship with channel partners is to assess their needs and try to align goals and objectives. The next step is to motivate resellers to attain the

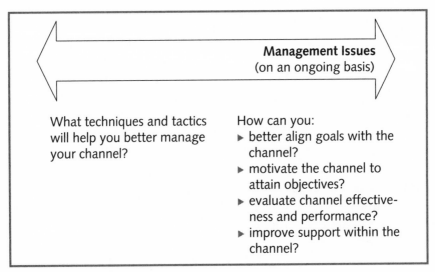

Management Issues
(on an ongoing basis)

What techniques and tactics will help you better manage your channel?

How can you:
- better align goals with the channel?
- motivate the channel to attain objectives?
- evaluate channel effectiveness and performance?
- improve support within the channel?

figure 1-3. Management issues

agreed-upon goals and provide appropriate support. The final step is to evaluate reseller performance so that you can take corrective action if it is needed.

Goal Alignment

As mentioned earlier in this chapter, some resellers carry substantial inventory volume while others focus on technical support as part of their business model. Manufacturers cannot expect an independent firm to change its strategic orientation for one principal unless it is beneficial for its overall business.

Therefore, the first step in goal alignment is ensuring that the resellers' business models fit the strategic goals of the manufacturer. After the "right" channels or channel members are determined, realistic and mutually agreed upon goals need to be established for product support and the various services and functions required for the products and customers in question.

Computer Associates, an Islandia, New York, company, tries to facilitate this type of goal alignment. It requests brief business plans from its channel partners and sets mutual expectations on the amount of investment and revenue expected from both sides.[14] Other companies might establish goals for customer satisfaction, repeat business, or follow-up service.

Motivating Channel Members

After goals are jointly established, channel managers must work to entice resellers to move toward attaining those goals. At minimum, distributors and other intermediaries want quality products that "fit" their businesses, acceptable inventory (or stocking) policies, adequate compensation, manufacturer follow-through on promises, and mutual trust. Beyond that—to stimulate shorter-term sales—discounts, sales promotions, and guarantees might be used.

Several types of discounts may be appropriate for the channel: volume discounts, long-term contracts, and functional discounts.

Volume discounts provide additional financial incentives for buying larger quantities, either for a given order (noncumulative) or over time (cumulative). They may be appropriate for commodity items requiring intensive distribution and immediate availability. However, they reward distributors on how they *buy* rather than how they *sell*.

Cumulative discounts, as well as long-term contracts, attempt to tie a channel member to your firm over time. Long-term contracts could include a flat price (balancing highs and lows in a turbulent price market such as energy transmission) or guarantee no price increases over a given time period.

Functional discounts are fees given to channel members performing specific services. Sometimes called activity-based compensation, functional discounts are appropriate when your product requires specific supporting services (e.g., a showroom, installation services, etc.) to be effective in the market.

Sales promotions include activities intended to spur sales in the short term. These can be used to encourage channel members to exceed assigned quotas, bolster slow sales seasons, move slow-moving products, reach new customers, or sell new products.

Contests, for example, may be used to generate excitement for a new product launch. The choice of a prize may be difficult because not all distributors value the same things. Therefore, some companies use "cafeteria incentive programs," allowing the channel members to choose their own prizes. Prizes could include free or partially reimbursed training, additional advertising allowances, free merchandise, and greater cooperative advertising latitude, in addition to trips and cash.

Prizes can also be more creative, as was the case with Evans Industries, a Detroit-based manufacturer of industrial products. At the time the firm was brainstorming a cost-effective way to stimulate distributor sales, the California lottery was up to $20 million. Evans Industries "bought a couple hundred lottery tickets and sent them to distributors along with a personal letter ... claiming they could be millionaires either by winning the lottery or selling [Evans] products."[15]

Guarantees made to end customers sometimes make it easier for distributors to sell products. This is particularly true for extended warranties on new products. Spiffs (sales promotion incentive funds) are additional compensation dollars given to reseller salespeople for selling a given manufacturer's product rather than competitive products. However, care must be taken to avoid causing salespeople to sell to customers where the product fit is questionable because that may harm long-term brand equity.

Support Tools and Programs

A crucial component in managing channels is ensuring that the support infrastructure (tools and programs to help channel members succeed) is in place. Major categories include promotional support, sales and technical support, and training.

Promotional support includes both *pull* strategies, which are designed to encourage end customers to pull product through the channel, and *push* strategies, which attempt to encourage channel members to push the product down to the customers.

Pull strategies include the advertising, public relations, and trade show activities the manufacturer performs to gain awareness of and preference for its products and brands. This is particularly important when channel motivation is low and/or pulling in new customers can reenergize channel interest. For example, national advertising and public relations, trade show attendance, press releases, and Web site information can encourage customers to seek out channels for the product or service, thereby encouraging more interest among channel members.

Push strategies include the support provided to encourage resellers to develop stronger ties with their customers, such as promotional funds (promotional allowances and cooperative advertising), customer promotions, and collateral material. Promotional allowances refer to rebates or monies given to resellers for their own local marketing. Cooperative advertising is a sharing of the cost of advertising when the channel member advertises the manufacturer's product. Both are typically percentages of the sales of a manufacturer's product, and both attempt to encourage resellers to generate demand at the local level. Customer promotions, such as local rebates, special deals, and customer contests, help channel members move more product.

Collateral materials can be designed to sell both *to* and *through* the channel. Material directed to the channel should emphasize the benefits they receive, e.g., increased throughput, ease of doing business, or greater profitability.

For material provided to the channel for use with customers, emphasis should be placed on end-customer benefits. This type of "pass-through" literature should be flexible enough for individual distributors and dealers to adapt with their contact information before they supply them to customers. Sometimes the simplest method is to provide the channel with templates that can be updated quickly. This is relevant even if the intermediary is a doctor, contractor, or other referring channel member.

Pass-through material might consist of preprinted direct mailers, kits, ad slicks, catalogs, product sheets, videos, bulletins, and CDs. Channel managers should incorporate brand identity guidelines where appropriate.

Sales and technical support programs are also part of the support infrastructure. Channel partners may require help in closing sales through team or joint sales calls, or assistance in solving customers' technical issues. This will be particularly true in large, complex selling situations, but even in less technical situations, channel members may benefit from extranet connections or 24-hour call centers. At minimum, channel managers should determine which type of channel requires what level of support.

The final aspect of support infrastructure is training, including both product training and skills training. Product training provides channel members with baseline knowledge of the features, benefits and competitive positioning of the manufacturer's products. Skills training focuses on specific skills, such as sales, marketing, business management or inventory management. Sales training helps channel partners understand *how to sell* the products of the manufacturer.

Marketing training educates channel partners on advertising basics, merchandising approaches, POP (point-of-purchase) displays, cross-selling opportunities, and communications policies that can result in improved performance.

Business training can provide direction on strategy, succession planning, contract issues, and financial management. Inventory training can help distributors with forecasting, replenishment, and control of stock. All of these approaches are designed to improve channel performance.

Performance Measurement

The success of a channel depends on monitoring its performance, getting solid feedback, and taking corrective action as necessary. In general, each channel member should be evaluated on how well the goals mentioned earlier have been attained. But such evaluation requires that the most appropriate metrics be identified. It's important that performance measures are used consistently across channel members and that channel members understand the metrics and commit to collecting and providing the relevant information.

Getting channel feedback is also important for staying close to the end customer, identifying potential areas of improvement, and maintaining trust. Channel feedback can be attained through formal and informal surveys or leadership councils made up of select distributors (for a distributor advisory council) or select reps (for a rep advisory council). These groups provide input on new product ideas, market shifts, and recommended process changes.

Reflection Point

Do I use the best techniques to manage my channel?
- ▶ Do I understand my channel partners' business models and try to capitalize on them rather than change them?
- ▶ Do I establish realistic goals for the channel?
- ▶ Are discounts structured in a way to motivate desired behavior on the part of distributors?
- ▶ Are sales promotions restricted to short-term incentives?
- ▶ Is a solid support infrastructure in place to manage the channel?
- ▶ Have I developed concrete and appropriate performance measures for the channel?

Stages of Channel Redesign

Individuals involved in channel strategy must be aware of both the strategic (planning) and management (implementation) issues of channel design. The remainder of this book brings these issues together by following the phases of channel redesign listed in Figure 1-4.

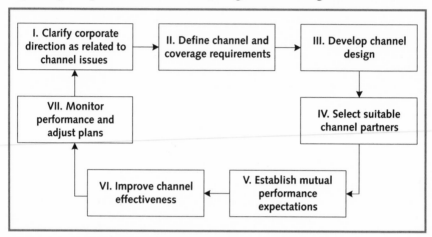

Figure 1-4. Stages of channel redesign

The following three chapters provide an executive overview of distribution issues and correspond to Stage I: clarify corporate direction as related to distribution. Chapter 2 on "forces shaping distribution strategy" expands on the factors of strategic fit introduced in Chapter 1, highlighting what is occurring in the business world today that may cause firms to rethink their distribution strategies. One significant change that can affect distribution strategy is the emergence of supply chain management, as discussed in Chapter 3. The philosophy of supply chain management forces managers to think about competitive advantage from a broader perspective—beyond just their own firm—improving the flow of product from raw material to end user. Chapter 4 provides an introduction to the legal issues of distributor-manufacturer relations with a focus on the strategy of prevention rather than litigation.

Part Two on strategic decisions corresponds with the next three phases of the model. Chapter 5 examines a multitude of issues related to defining channel and coverage requirements (Stage II), including both proactive and reactive measures as well as a sample distributor satisfaction questionnaire template. Chapters 6 and 7 focus on developing channel design (Stage III). Chapter 6 addresses domestic design issues, and Chapter 7 deals with international issues. Chapter 8 discusses how to select suitable channel partners (Stage IV).

Part Three on managing the ongoing relationship corresponds with the remaining phases of the process. Chapter 9 on understanding the distributor's world and Chapter 10 on establishing mutual performance expectations link with Stage V. Chapter 11 on designing and implementing programs provides a hands-on perspective for accomplishing Stage VI. Finally, Chapter 12 helps with the final step of monitoring performance and adjusting plans accordingly (Stage VII).

Key Points

▶ Stay abreast of changes in the way your customers want to buy your type of product.
▶ Creatively explore new go-to-market approaches.
▶ Determine whether modifications in distribution may be necessary due to market transformations, strategy shifts, new product launches and/or changes in product and market requirements.
▶ Maintain control of your brand equity throughout your channels.
▶ Try to reduce channel conflict by offering different product versions through different channels.
▶ Align your goals and objectives with channel objectives.
▶ Provide appropriate motivational incentives to the channel.
▶ Ensure that a solid support infrastructure is in place.
▶ Measure performance and be prepared to take corrective action as necessary.

Notes

1. Gary McWilliams, "In About-Face, Dell Will Sell PCs to Dealers," *Wall Street Journal*, 20 August 2002, p. B1.
2. Alicia Zappier, "Avon to Unveil new Cosmetics Line at Sears, Penney Beauty Centers," *Drug Store News*, 30 October 2000, p. 39.

3. Louis W. Stern, Adel I. El-Ansary, and Anne T. Coughlan, *Marketing Channels*, 5th ed., (Upper Saddle River, NJ: Prentice Hall, 1996), p. 1.
4. Ibid, p. 26
5. Donna Fuscaldo, "Looking Big," *Wall Street Journal*, 28 April 2003, p. R7.
6. Jennifer Kuhel, "Attention Wal-Mart Suppliers," *Supply Chain Technology News*, November 2002, Web site: www.supplychain-tech.com.
7. John R. Hall, "Honeywell Launches Online Contractor Services Program," *Air Conditioning, Heating & Refrigeration News,* 12 August 2002, pp. 29-32.
8. Trevor Thomas, "Nationwide to Distribute through CPAs," *National Underwriter,* 20 May 2002, pp. 16-17.
9. Trevor Thomas, "And the Distribution Winners Are ..." *National Underwriter,* 12 November 2001, pp. 88-91.
10. James P. Morgan, "No More Magic," *Purchasing,* 1 May 2003, pp. 17-21.
11. James Narus and James Anderson, "Rethinking Distribution: Adaptive Channels," *Harvard Business Review,* July-August 1996, p. 114.
12. Christopher Power, "Flops," *Business Week*, 16 August 1993, p. 79.
13. Lambeth Hochwald, "Tuning in to the Right Channel," *Sales and Marketing Management,* March 2000, pp. 66-74.
14. Julie Chang, "Grab Your Partner," *Sales and Marketing Management,* July 2002, p. 59.
15. Shari Caudron, "Guerrilla Tactics," *Industry Week,* 16 July 2001, p. 54.

Chapter 2

FORCES SHAPING CHANNEL STRATEGY

Business planning processes typically address a few fundamental questions. Where am I now (your situation analysis)? Where do I want to go (your goals)? How can I get there (your plan to close the gap between where you are and where you want to go)? What do I need to do it (the resources and support required for you to execute your plan and the tracking metrics you will use)?

The next three chapters help you think about the first two questions and relate your overall corporate initiatives to channel issues. In other words, you will begin to address the first stage in the channel design and refinement process by exploring the internal and external forces shaping distribution strategy (see Figure 2-1).

Channel Strategy as Part of Overall Business Strategy

Stage I makes a case for clarifying corporate direction in channel planning and execution. In this chapter, we encourage you to investigate and refine your present channels of distribution strategies and business plans. Plans built upon emerging challenges and forces are critical in getting your products to personal and/or business consumers or end users—the "ultimate consumers."

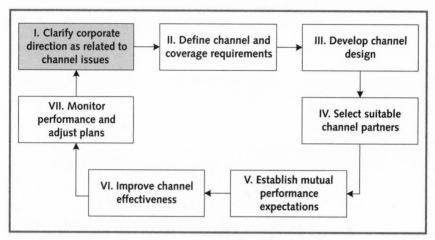

Figure 2-1. Stage I in channel redesign

Figure 2-2 depicts a generic strategy development process. Because channel strategy should be part of overall corporate strategy, it's useful to review the basic components. A starting point, as depicted in Figure 2-2, is to analyze the current situation. Assess the key business forces impacting future operations by conducting a situational assessment of internal and external forces. Be prepared to communicate any assumptions you have made.

Although the bulk of this chapter will cover the situation analysis discussed in the preceding paragraph, this section will address the remainder of the flowchart for business and channel strategy development. Here are some fundamental questions you should help your firm address as part of the "as is" business scenario.

- ▶ What are the firm's primary business strategies, and how does channel strategy complement and support other strategies?
- ▶ Is the firm striving to improve operational excellence by fine-tuning internal processes to eliminate waste and cut costs? Is the firm trying to be the low cost producer in its industry?
- ▶ Is the firm striving to be more customer-centric, even end-user/consumer-centric in developing strategy?
- ▶ Is the firm striving to grow through product management objectives such as rationalizing the present product line and focusing upon "A" and "B" high-volume items?

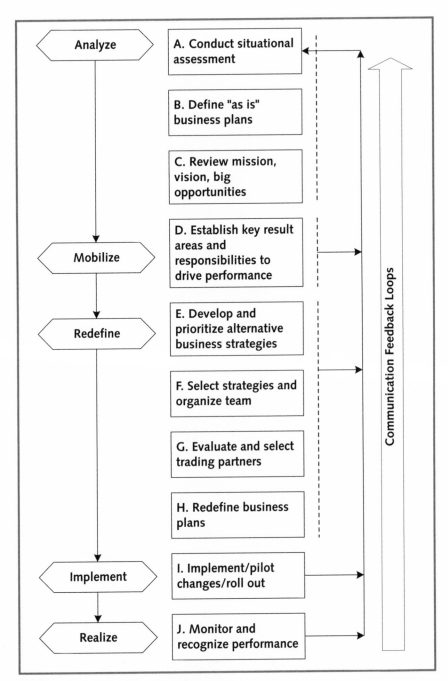

Figure 2-2. Strategy development

▶ Is product life-cycle management a driving force for managing new product introductions, accelerating growth products, and managing end-of-life product changes?

▶ Is the firm attempting to grow Outside USA (OUSA) business, which is often driven by big customers?

▶ Is the firm striving to grow through mergers or acquisitions?

While appraising business forces and analyzing as-is business scenarios, review your present mission and vision (see Step C of Figure 2-2). The mission statement defines why the firm exists—what is its basic purpose? The vision statement indicates where top management wants to direct the firm to be, for instance, in three years.

Is there a difference between the as-is situation and the vision for the future? Putting it another way, if the firm were to take a snapshot picture of the firm at time point A and compare it to a desired snapshot three years into the future, what critical business forces might impact the viability of closing the gap?

Some firms have found, for example, that channel changes are necessary to reach the long-term goals that are part of the vision. It's become almost trendy to sell through other firm's channels—to form alliances that provide mutual benefits. When Sears acquired Lands' End in 2002, there were advantages for both organizations. Sears gained a respected brand of clothing, and Lands' End extended its market reach through Sears' outlets. However, the changes in channel strategy were part of changes in business strategies for both organizations.

There are other examples of firms that have found it necessary to modify channel strategy to accomplish long-term corporate goals. A distributor has as its mission to be a sole-source distributor of maintenance, repair, and operating (MRO) items for selected industrial original equipment manufacturers (OEMs). Its vision is to grow the firm in three years from $250 million to $500 million and to have major market share in North America. To accomplish its vision, it will be necessary to establish strong relationships with both customers and relevant suppliers who will support the distributor in its initiatives.

Another example involves a manufacturer whose vision was to double the firm's sales from $500 million to $1 billion in three years and for 40 percent of its sales to be OUSA. To attain the vision, several possible strategies should be explored. New product lines with high growth potential could be pursued. Another strategy could be to merge with an OUSA company in the European Union (EU) that has major market presence, complementary product lines, and country presence with a solid distributor base. Rather than developing international strategies from scratch, the manufacturer takes advantage of the merged firm's EU presence, and the EU firm takes advantage of the other firm's U.S. presence.

Continuing with Figure 2-2, note that Step D addresses key result areas as targets for growth and improvement. A focus on the key result areas helps mobilize efforts toward change. In the two cases above, revenue growth and international presence were two key areas in which performance was to be assessed and recognized. Both of these targets affect and are affected by channel strategy.

Next, the firm may need to redefine its strategies and plans. As listed in steps E and F, it must prioritize alternative business strategies and then select the one or two major strategies for which the firm will redesign the business and modify operations.

Steps G and H then require the firm to pick key trading partners up and down the channel and negotiate beneficial relationships.

Step I deals with implementation and the critical rollout of new strategy. How is the firm going to implement business and associated channel strategies discussed in this book? Finally, in step J, results are analyzed with various parties recognized. If the firm has spent time defining key result areas and how to evaluate performance in Step D of Figure 2-2, then this measurement and recognition should come easier. Award programs, in addition to or in place of cash, are excellent means for recognizing performance.

Reflection Point

Does my business strategy link to my channel strategy?

▶ How well does my channel strategy support and complement the overall corporate strategy?

▶ Is it consistent with the mission and vision?

▶ Are key result areas specified and adhered to?

External Forces Impacting Channel Strategy

As mentioned earlier in the chapter, sound business strategies are built on a solid situational assessment, and channel strategies are no exception. Therefore, it's useful to highlight some of the critical external forces that must be considered in channel evaluation.

Increased Attention on the End User

Where should you start? Start with the end customer—your firm's biggest asset! An end-user orientation is a big factor in business growth, improved profitability for channel trading partners, and even survival in some cases. A basic goal of businesses today is to know what is happening in the front lines (in addition to gathering information on a second-hand or third-hand basis from intermediate customers). The further a firm is from end users, the more difficult it is to determine what is happening in the usage of its product and service offerings.

Demand as represented in purchase orders from channel customers reflects many policies, procedures and practices relative to how they process orders and how they relate to suppliers. These customer-ordering methods affect order quantities but may not actually represent usage information or what is required to help the end customer make a buying decision.

Companies have occasionally tried to push their end customers to buy from the "wrong" types of channels—primarily because it was easier for the manufacturer. Many companies during the early stages of e-commerce, for example, tried to save money by enticing their customers to buy online—only to discover that not all customers were comfortable with this approach. Some wanted a single source supplier for a variety of complementary products. Others wanted local product availability and credit services. Still others wanted installation and ongoing maintenance and support.

Manufacturers have begun to reexamine the distribution functions and services necessary to satisfy end-customer needs. The Huffy Cross Sport case described in Chapter 1 provides an example. The hybrid bike required a more structured selling approach than was possible in the firm's traditional channel partners such as Kmart and Toys R Us. Since there was no *selling* per se, customers did not understand the benefits of the new product.

You can gather the necessary information in several ways. One is to *observe* customer behavior. Visit your distributors, dealers, or retailers to determine the relative importance of demonstrations, showrooms, displays, etc., in helping end customers make purchase decisions. Ride along on sales calls to assess the "fit" of the channel partner in satisfying customer needs.

Survey customers not only on their satisfaction with your products and services but also on their expectations of and satisfaction with your channels. Ask them about their preferences toward any channel modifications you are considering.

You may also be able to test possible channel changes through market experiments. For example, if you are considering adding (or deleting) showrooms, test the change in a territory or region before making the change in all locations. You may want to refer to a basic marketing research book as you begin work on this project.[1]

Increased Attention to the Channel Partner

Companies have found that even with a superior product, strong marketing communications, and a fair price, market share can drop when there is insufficient attention provided to channel partners. Companies may spend millions of dollars launching a new product, but comparatively minimal amounts to launch a new channel.

Very often, the dealers and/or distributors are treated with benign neglect. CNH Group (formerly Case New Holland) learned the importance of channel management after suffering a 30-percent share erosion in a key market. Its research showed little difference in the way buyers of compact tractors (its end users) rated its brands versus competitive brands. However, the research also showed that the top value driver for end users was the dealer relationship. Further *channel* research showed that *dealers* gave New Holland lower scores than the competition on benefits the manufacturer could provide to *them*. This pointed out the relationship attributes New Holland needed to fix.[2]

Who are your partner customers? What is happening to your customer base? Certainly, market segmentation and customer grouping are now being carried to new levels of investigation and determination. Are your partner customers treated as a generic glob with little discrimination as to required services, or do you serve customers on a personal basis? As an example, do you serve customers with little discrimination as to who gets what services and when—customers receive first-come, first-serve treatment and are allocated product from whatever is in stock to be delivered next day if the orders are received by 2:00 p.m. today?

In today's environment of specialized customer needs, it is not unusual for firms to segment their partner customers into as many as 100 segments requiring a broad menu of services. Different distributors can have very different needs as discussed in later chapters. Are current channel policies relevant and sufficient to meet these broad customer service performance requirements in today's marketplace?

Assessing Needs of Partner Customers

Below are some dimensions and considerations for assessing needs and in segmenting your partner customers based on these needs. Many of these questions lead to channel strategies incorporating a menu of services with price and ultimate cost differentials. In reviewing the following questions, reflect upon the menu of product and service pricing and promotional incentives options by channel.

These channel differentials address how customers define their needs and participate in manufacturer offerings relative to demand creation and demand fulfillment requests. The following are questions to consider in segmenting and grouping partner customers.

▶ Who are your direct customers? If you are a battery manufacturer, you may sell through traditional channels (such as mass merchandisers, retail food chains, industrial distributors and surgical supply distributors), as well as OEMs who include batteries with end products for resale (such as toy manufacturers, medical devices, and watches). What are the different requirements by channel?

▶ Do specific customers have an extensive list of policies as to (a) how products are packaged, labeled, and assorted for resale or use, (b) the need for reusable containers, or (c) requirements for unitized load requirements, paperwork, transportation pickups?

▶ Does marketing approach segmentation both from the perspective of end users and direct customers?

▶ How many customers do you have by market segment?

▶ What is the market potential of evaluated segments—revenue potential and willingness to spend money on your products and services?

▶ What is happening in the size of customers? In today's environment of economic concentration within market segments, it is not unusual to have five "A-1" customers who account for 50 percent of the sales by channel. One customer may even account for 25 to 90 percent of a firm's business! What are the consequences of these economic developments on your channel selection, management, and personnel commitments?

▶ Are certain customers driving/pulling you to new business? As they grow, or diminish, or exit, what impact are they having on your business?

▶ What promotional requirements are placed upon manufacturers?

▶ What different requirements will you face with foreign suppliers and/or channel members?

Changes within specific channels can also dictate potential changes in your strategies, or at least cause you to keep a wary eye open. The automotive industry, for example is experiencing some dealer transformations. Big auto malls are making a resurgence, with an emphasis on "destination car shopping." The North Scottsdale Auto Mall near Phoenix has "two test tracks, a racing museum, a café that serves Starbucks, and almost a dozen car brands under one roof."[3] Many car manufacturers are discouraging the growth of this channel because they would prefer not to have their products side by side with competitors, but it is the ultimate consumers who will determine whether this go-to-market strategy makes sense.

Demographics of Population

The U.S. population is growing more diverse, and that is manifesting itself in both the profile of customers and channel employees. The Hispanic-American population increased 58 percent between the 1990 and 2000 censuses, and—at 35 million—is larger than the entire population of Canada. With increasing population growth and participation rates, the share of minorities in the labor force is expected to expand substantially. The size of the labor force was 62 million in 1950. This jumped to nearly 141 million in 2000, with the growth rate of women in the labor force higher than that of men.[4]

Manufacturers will need to design products, channels, and support services that meet the needs of these diverse audiences. This may require packaging, labeling and documentation in more than one language and training and motivation appropriate for specific ethnic groups. Economic per capita income and spending patterns must be assessed in relation to the distribution channel's potential sales and order fulfillment.

Three fundamental areas in assessing market potential leading to selected channels are (1) how many people are in segments being considered; (2) do they have money—average per capita income; and (3) are they able and willing to spend their money for your product/service offering—and not just once but on a repetitive basis?

Other countries are also experiencing demographic shifts. Many have had a surge in the middle class, opening up markets for several goods—as long as manufacturers make appropriate modifications in strategy. Amway, for example, is now doing well in China. After door-to-door pyramid selling (the model used by Amway) was declared illegal by the Chinese government, Amway opened up retail stores. In 2003 there were about 100 such outlets, with China being its number four market worldwide.[5]

There may also need to be changes that reflect the younger generations' higher comfort with technology. Whereas Web sites and e-mail are now commonplace in business, Instant Messaging (IM) is still the domain of consumer teenagers. However, analysts expect that to change. The consulting firm Gartner estimates that IM will overtake e-mail as the primary communications tool at work.[6] In fact, IM handles are how turning up on business cards.[7] If end customers begin to expect that type of communication for customer service or technical support, manufacturers will need to be prepared to handle it either directly or through their channels.

The Splintering of Channels!

The demise of distributors has not occurred. Rather, one of the big areas of opportunity is how manufacturing and distributor operations are codeveloping. Instead of the demise of distributors as many predicted when the "dot-com" era was booming in the late 1990s, many distributor organizations have become stronger. Economic factors have led to increased industry concentration with distributors merging to gain market power and efficiencies.

For one manufacturer, with which an author of this book consulted, a U.S. distributor network that was 500-plus locations is now owned by 85 companies with properties not necessarily geographically adjacent. As the economy and business relationships changed, distributors began buying each other up. For another firm, in just three years, five distributors grew to 50 percent of the supplier's business.

There are several examples of distributors that have grown to be full-service vendors for their customers. Some large industrial distributors have begun to manage the inventory of their customers through supplier or vendor managed inventory (SMI or VMI) programs.

W. W. Grainger, for example, has become a single source pipeline for many companies ranging in size from the very small to very large, multinational firms. Surgical supply dealers, such as Owens & Minor, distribute a complete line of finished goods to hospitals and clinics for servicing patients.

However, the demands of some large customers on manufacturers are causing a splintering of traditional business channels. Many suppliers are now managing an increasing diversity of go-to-market strategies, some of which include bypassing distributors and going direct to retailers and end users. Large (greater than $1 billion) "business/industrial" customers are demanding that suppliers serve them directly; e.g., OEMs and capital goods' buyers are bypassing industrial and specialized distributors.

Certainly the Internet has been a major force in this splintering of channels. Many suppliers are going directly to large A-1 national and international accounts. Other customers in the remaining "A, B, and C" categories continue to be serviced by distributors. Where large concentrations of midsize customers exist, as in the medical services field, distributors are a major force in the pipeline for getting a supplier's goods to these customers.

As concentration in the distributor segment of our business channels occurs, streamlined and diverse channels and supply chains are becoming the norm and not the exception. In some situations where the presale and negotiation activities are direct between manufacturer and customer, the distributor channel is taking the lead in postsale activities.

In other situations, manufacturers are reaching out to nontraditional firms to provide services (e.g., technical support) when they sell directly to customers—to in effect create a hybrid channel, as will be discussed later. Distributor functionality is being assessed as part of "reintermediation" rather than "disintermediation"—or the demise—of the distributor.

In addition to the distributors playing a primary role in moving direct products and sales materials, they are playing an increasingly important role in servicing customers for *indirect* materials and services. These indirect materials include capital equipment; packaging, dunnage, returnable shipping containers; MRO supplies; janitorial services; reworked or refurbished items; recyclables; communications equipment; contract labor; energy and water supplies; aftermarket parts and supplies; and office supplies. The role of distributors in servicing these secondary needs is often more important than the primary product distribution channels. Each of the indirect supplies areas has associated networks of and linked channel trading partners of which distributors are playing major roles.

The demise of the distributor has not occurred.

Competition

What your competitors are doing to reach your customers could very well impact how you choose to go to market. But it is becoming increasingly difficult in some industries to define exactly who the competition is. Domestic competition is tough enough, but with foreign competition targeting business or personal consumers, foreign manufacturers are targeting your distributors to handle their products.

The impact is that manufacturers have to get out of the commodity game based upon price and seek to build stronger relationships with distributors and with product consumers. In the chapter on supply-chain management, you will learn about demand/usage management tactics and asset rationalization techniques to build strong relationships with users/consumers while aiding your distributors in becoming more profitable.

Part of these tactics will deal with drop shipping techniques that aid distributors in offering broader lines of products, similar to W. W. Grainger going from some 90,000 SKU offerings to some 225,000 offerings through streamlined channels of supply to meet the broad needs of its customers. A responsibility of manufacturing suppliers is to keep abreast of competitive strategies and tactics in relation to direct and indirect end-user marketing activities.

Government Regulations

In many industries (such as in banking, communications and transportation) aspects of government and economic regulations have been greatly relaxed, with more reliance on market forces than on government regulations. However, in safety and security issues, regulations have been tightened. "People" regulations, along with the safe production, handling, and movement of goods have been tightened and increased. Because many regulations are industry specific, they will not be listed here. This section is simply included as a reminder to consider these factors in the design of channel strategy.

In relation to foreign countries and the World Trade Organization, relevant regulations must be addressed in developing global business strategy. A case in point is the EU where in the past manufacturers went through distributors to reach consumers. With the relaxation of EU intercountry trade laws and regulations, many firms are now going direct to users and buying out distributors. These firms have selected key marketing and distribution points, such as in the Netherlands, to directly move their products to their destinations.

Other distributor functions are being assumed by manufacturers as they develop direct and agent relationships with foreign nationals. In this case, disintermediation of distributor channels forces the supplier to assume much of the functionality previously provided by distributors.

Conservation and the Environment

A separate area of regulation and environmental consciousness is related to our global resources. Governments have instigated additional regulations in this area requiring suppliers to make decisions on environmental policies for both their internal operations as well as their trading partners. How does the supplier implement environmental policies within its enterprise as well as require its trading partners to abide by corporate and/or government regulations?

As the firm assesses its mission, vision, and strategic intent, responses to how the firm and its distributors deal with these regulations can put the organization in either a positive or negative competitive position. Can the firm treat environmental consciousness as a means to competitive advantage? Many of these environmental issues can be utilized in building competitive advantage and in building stockholder value.

For example, medical equipment manufacturers who take ownership of old equipment, or automobile battery manufacturers who invest in recycling programs use environmental issues to create competitive advantage.

In summary, you must identify, assess the impact, and prioritize the above external forces to pick those that will play a critical part in determining channel strategy and business outcome.

Reflection Point

Do I take a broad look at external forces in the assessment of channel direction?

▶ Have I ever tried to "force fit" a channel because it was easier?

▶ Do I collect information from customers and channel partners on their level of satisfaction with my firm?

▶ How well do I monitor competitors' go-to-market strategies?

▶ Have I prepared for channel splintering, demographic shifts, and governmental initiatives in channel design?

Internal Forces Shaping Channel Strategy

Besides contemplating external forces, you must address internal strategic initiatives and assess the impact of these forces on channel strategy. These internal areas of policy and strategy provide the "momentum" from previously established plans, policies, and procedures—leading to new or modified goals and strategies.

Customer and Trading Partner Relationship Management

The preceding discussion of customer diversity points to the challenges facing manufacturers today. The increased use of customer relationship management (CRM) and supplier relationship management (SRM) processes to establish and manage points of contact between customers and suppliers is receiving much attention. On the customer side, sales and customer service representatives were historically the primary company representatives in contact with customers.

Now firms are going from single points of contact to "team" contacts on behalf of sellers and buyers and, in some cases, other intermediaries. These inter-enterprise, cross-functional teams are modifying business practices to meet end-user demand while achieving improved returns from invested or deployed resources. Because of limited resources, team relationships typically focus upon a select few, large, direct customers, as well as large distributors who, in turn, are responsible for serving the manufacturer's smaller customers.

Product Development and Management

As mentioned earlier, the selling and servicing requirements of products should have an impact on channel strategy. Manufacturers who include innovation in their mission and vision statements will likely be active in new product development and bring out truly new products on an ongoing basis. Products that are new to the world and require extensive customer education necessitate channels that provide that functionality. Therefore, these types of manufacturers will need to build educational competencies into their channel strategies to be effective.

As products move through the life cycle, requiring less "selling," manufacturers may need to move to more "self-service" channels to accommodate the changing customer requirements. The provision of parts and servicing may be required of those channels, even if active selling is not.

For many products with a long life, the availability of aftermarket parts poses a challenge for manufacturers. If a product is declining (and profitability going down), manufacturers will strive for low-cost channels, and eventually either sell, license or outsource the product servicing for the remainder of the product's life. Channel members should be kept in the loop as these decisions are being made.

Manufacturing/Operations Developments

Postponing manufacturing and/or assembly operations until further down the channel closer to end users is becoming common. A local furniture store, focusing on oak and other wood products, established an assembly operation for dining room tables. By carrying a specific number of leg and tabletop styles, the store was able to inventory the legs and tops as individual stock units, rather than warehousing every combination of leg and tabletop as final table units. The result was less space taken up in inventory, as well as faster response to customer requests for tables.

A related strategy is the technical substitution of product ingredients or components to enhance profitability and become a stronger competitor. The following five examples demonstrate some of these phenomena, which are dramatically impacting channel design:

Film processing and picture development. Film is being processed in retail outlets—and with the advent of digital imagery— pictures are now processed electronically and printed in homes and businesses. The nature of specialty firms to service these markets have changed dramatically for manufacturers of imaging equipment and supplies. The whole industry is being transformed as pictures can be transmitted electronically around the world.

Many product ingredients are being synthetically produced. For instance, vanilla used in cooking is now chemically produced instead of being extracted from beans. Milk is coming from soybeans. Fuel is coming from corn.

Colors are impregnated into products, which is less costly and better on the environment but may also require changes in channel flows and services.

Products, such as foods and kitty litter, are packaged and labeled closer to use. These products are shipped in bulk and then packaged and labeled locally or regionally, often with automatic identification symbology, to meet customer and end-user differentiated needs.

Durable goods parts, such as automotive parts, are being locally recycled, refurbished and put back into the business stream, thus helping profits and lessening harmful effects upon the environment. New channels have emerged to meet these needs.

Impact of Information Technologies

The previous discussion leads to the impact of information technologies. Table 2-1 identifies a variety of information technologies (IT) and related processing systems. As illustrated in the table, IT goes beyond e-commerce, which has received most of the buzz lately. With the use of processes to keep track of and even to manage end-usage of products, this broad set of information technologies must be monitored in order to gain competitive advantage or even avoid being put out of business.

The intent is not to be on the "bleeding edge" in the use of many, available technologies but to be aware of the potential for using this broad array of products. These technologies are particularly important in maintaining viable supplier-distributor relationships in which an increasing amount of information is being exchanged between business trading partners.

With the concentration in the distributor segment of channels, distributors are becoming larger. These larger distributors are demanding the use of IT for marketing, operations, purchasing, and logistics control. The final point of the critical nature of this discussion about IT is that you must be abreast of these advancements to maintain your competitive posture and to improve the retention and management of distributors. The following box provides an overview of IT tools for business tactics and execution.

Data coding and structures ANSI, EDIFACT, CPFR, data identifiers

Data capture and collection keyboard, bar coding, smart cards, RFID, OCR, imaging, voice, RFDC, satellite, GPS and GsIT

Database managers portable, front-end controllers, main-frame, GIS, ERP, SC VANs

Electronic commerce for B2B or B2C—EDI, Internet, XML, CRT/Extranet, direct links, ASPs

---

Decision-aiding tools for strategic and tactical planning and control

Management reporting Tabular, graphical, control charts, and GIS geographical maps for performance analysis

Note: Definition of Acronyms

ANSI American National Standards Institute oversees the approval of Approved Standards Committees (ASCs) for interest groups to establish standards.

EDIFACT Electronic Data Interchange for Approved Commercial Transactions for international standards.

Data Interchange Standards Association (DISA) is secretariat for domestic and international standards for EDI and Internet standards. www.disa.org.

CPFR Collaborative Planning, Forecasting and Replenishment for coordinated planning and forecasting.

RFID Radio Frequency Identification "tags" to identify entities.

RFDC Radio Frequency Data Collection to capture data through radio frequencies.

OCR and ICR Optical or Intelligent Character Recognition by capturing data from images.

Global Positioning Systems (GPS) and Geo-spatial Information Technologies (GsIT) to capture data on global sourcing bases.

Geographic Information Systems (GIS) to process globally based data.

Enterprise Resource Planning (ERP) systems to centrally house and process enterprise-wide data.

Supply Chain Value-Added Networks to capture and process supply chain-wide data.

Business-to-Business (B2B) and **Business-to-Consumer (B2C) EDI and XLM** Internet exchanges to capture and process inter-enterprise or inter-enterprise/consumer data.

CRT dial-up or Extranet limited access, secured data bases for business customers and suppliers to access a firm's enterprise systems.

Application Services Provider (ASP) Internet-based software for external parties to access, input data, and process for actionable information.

To briefly explain how to use the six areas of IT listed above, consider the opportunities for building databases of information for use by persons in your firm or for use with your trading partners. Where should you start? Start with defining basic time stamped, transaction sets, and associated data requirements.

Process map what your employees are doing now—noting transactions, paper, and information flows. How are data coded for data transmission and storage? As firms aspire to do electronic exchange of business data, the adoption of business-to-business communications standards is critical to efficient and effective data processing.

Many means exist to electronically capture the data and transmit the data into computer databases besides keyboarding for data manipulation and analysis. Automatic product and transactional identification—including the use of bar coding, imaging, and radio-frequency identification (RFID) of orders, shipments, and inventories—is critical.

Databases can be located at places where events first take place (in remote or portable computers), or they can be stored on Internet servers with Web-based application service packages. No longer do you need to have computer-resident software.

Electronic communications can occur using fax, traditional electronic data interchange (EDI), or over the Internet for business-to-business communications. Decision-aiding tools help you make better decisions strategically and tactically as you plan future activities. Many services and software packages are now available to aid you in "mining" the data for exceptions to improve operations and productivity.

Organizational Developments

A key force affecting organizations is the role of outsourcing functionality to present or new trading partners or to other third-party providers. Functional specialists have evolved to the point that some parties have discussed the existence of virtual organizations that command and control outsourced functional providers. What cannot be outsourced—from basic research to financial settlements of orders? Where "disintermediation" was initially presented as an approach in which trading partners, such as distributors, were to be eliminated, now "reintermediation" is being addressed in relation to which trading partners can best perform certain tasks such as the following:

- ▶ modular product design, involving tasks in which present trading partners need to collaborate with outside product design specialists
- ▶ demand forecasting and operations scheduling across the channel directed at end users and collaboratively among manufacturers, distributors, and other channel trading partners. Industries in this category include retail chains, food service dis-

tributors, medical equipment and supplies, and office supplies.
- ► logistics fulfillment tasks assumed by new third-party logistics services providers.

Trading partners are taking value engineering and analysis to a new level in analyzing inter-enterprise functionality rather than dis-intermediating partners entirely. These organizational considerations are discussed in more detail when channel design is addressed.

Finally, more emphasis is being devoted to developing balanced scorecards of enterprise and inter-enterprise performance measures. More than ever, there is a need to identify and define good metrics to measure performance beyond the financials. Later chapters address the need for good metrics to measure and recognize performance.

Human Resources Management Policies and Practices

Rising healthcare costs and a business focus on improved labor pro-ductivity have led to dramatic changes in how the performance of our employees are recognized and compensated. Levels of benefits beyond direct compensation are being scrutinized.

Organizational and employee loyalty are not as strong as in pre-vious years. Employees are not wedded to organizations as in the past, with the high majority of the workforce making more job and career changes. How do you manage dynamic work force changes plus deal with the increased outsourcing of functionality and labor itself? The use of contract labor is becoming more prevalent as organizations rely on outside experts to manage the labor force.

Suppliers and distributors must plan and manage human resource practices in these fluid labor situations. Another issue affecting channel management is the exchange or placement of sup-plier or customer employees on site at the other partner's location. All of these areas affect manufacturer/distributor relationships as organizations seek improved labor efficiency by cutting across organ-izations. Firms are increasingly sharing labor resources as they con-duct detailed reviews of job contributions.

Collaborative Strategic Alliances

Collaborative strategic alliances are an example of an outstanding development leading to collaborative relationships among trading partners. The development of integrated, collaborative supplier and distributor (i.e., vertical) relationships was discussed previously. Now horizontal collaborative relationships are developing relative to competitors and complementary suppliers. As buyers or sellers get larger, the aggregation of buying power across competitors is developing as a force to deal with.

Automobile manufacturers, through such organizations as COVISINT (an online buying organization), are pooling orders to buy in larger volumes for themselves directly or indirectly for their suppliers, such as steel and polymer companies. Pharmaceutical suppliers now must deal with large distributors who control the pipeline of supplies into hospitals. Competing companies must join forces through these distributors if they are to sell their products in the hospital industry.

Complementary distributors involving medical, safety, office, and power utilities supplies work together to gain tactical and transactional efficiencies from collaborative activities in servicing industries, such as petroleum pipeline companies. The bottom line is that if you want to do business in certain channels, collaboration is the name of the game.

Supply Chain Management

Related to collaborative business activities is the development of total end-end supply chain management processes that focus on end-user satisfaction. Chapter 3 will examine in detail this area of development in which supply chains of trading partners are competing with other supply chains in fulfilling end-user demand.

One of the goals of total end-end thinking is to respond to business or personal usage of products and services instead of considering only the derived demand between business partners. Supply chain economics is drawing increased attention as organizations

Reflection Point

How aware am I of internal forces that could impact channel strategy?

▶ Will future product changes require alternations in my go-to-market strategy?

▶ Can deferred assembly or postponement provide a competitive advantage?

▶ What technologies can be adapted from other industries or usages for an improvement in my channel?

realize that profitability goes beyond traditional micro- and macro-economics. Supply chain core processes that are based upon collaborative relationships are leading to new organizational and supply chain governance issues.

Key Points

▶ Be sure your channel strategy is consistent with your overall business initiatives.
▶ Think long-term with a consistent vision.
▶ Get closer to your end customers!
▶ Keep your eye on external and internal forces that may require modifications in your channel.
▶ Maintain a team orientation.
▶ Be a relationship builder—internally and externally.

Notes

1. To learn more about marketing research techniques, you may want to add a couple of books to your library. One is *The Market Research Toolbox: A Concise Guide for Beginners* (Sage Publications, 1996) by Edward McQuarrie. Because it includes topics such as developing a customer visit program, it goes beyond traditional survey design publications. Another book to consider, especially if your end customer is a consumer, is *How Customers Think: Essential Insights into the Mind of the Market* (Harvard Business School Press, 2003) by Gerald Zaltman.
2. Bob Donath, "Value Studies Reveal Insufficient Attention to Dealers Plenty Costly," *Marketing News*, 28 October 2002, pp. 8-9.
3. Karen Lundegaard, "Destination Car Shopping," *The Wall Street Journal*, 3 June 2003, p. B1.
4. Mitra Toossi, "A Century of Change: The U.S. Labor Force, 1950-2050," *Monthly Labor Review*, May 2002, pp. 15-28.
5. Leslie Chang, "Amway in China: Once Barred, Now Booming," *The Wall Street Journal*, 12 March 2003, pp. B1-B5.
6. Christine Y. Chen, "The IM Invasion," *Fortune*, 26 May 2003, pp. 135-138.
7. Jennifer Tanaka, "You 'Pinging' Me?" *Newsweek*, 12 May 2003, p. E12.

Chapter 3

SUPPLY CHAIN MANAGEMENT

Many manufacturers have traditionally shipped product out to their dealers and distributors with the attitude, "Now, Mr. Distributor, just go out and sell it." The dealer or distributor was considered *the customer*, without much thought about what happened to the product beyond that point.

Now companies are increasingly looking down the channel at their customer's customer and sometimes up the channel at their supplier's supplier. This thought process is the essence of supply chain management and is one of the forces shaping channel strategy today. Given the importance of supply chain issues in today's business, an entire chapter has been devoted to the topic.

Fulfilling the Demands of Supply Chain Trading Partners

Companies that are recognized as successful in supply chain implementation are also successful in the stock market, according to a multiyear research project conducted by Accenture, INSEAD, and Stanford University. The report, " A Global Study of Supply Chain Leadership and Its Impact on Business Performance," was based on data from more than 600 Global 3000 companies in 24 industries.[1]

As documented in the report,

> nearly 25% of all respondents cited *enhancing revenue* as their [supply chain] initiative's most prominent driver. Other drivers cited were reducing cost, reducing working capital, more margin potential.... In effect, service and support are becoming as important as the product itself. And supply chain management is the heart of profitable service and support.[2]

Other research by one of the authors provided input from manufacturers, wholesalers, distributors, retailers, and third-party intermediaries into this major study of the impact of supply chain management on business development. Supply chain management is a major force impacting channel design and management.

Many people think about supply chains in the context of technology improvements and cutting costs. And although that is part of the focus, companies also realize that there can be a variety of ways to be better than the competition at satisfying end-customer needs.

Speaking in a panel discussion on supply chains, Robert Porter Lynch, CEO of the Warren Company and author of *Business Alliances Guide: The Hidden Competitive Weapon*, said, "A principle in business is that you cut costs to survive, but you innovate to prosper."[3] Supply chain management should be as much about innovation as it is about cost cutting.

Getting Out of the Enterprise Box

In early stages of demand fulfillment, manufacturers traditionally focused their attention on managing the functional interactions and handoffs within the firm in demand planning, purchasing and supply management, manufacturing operations, and fulfillment processes. As they progressed in thinking outside of their enterprise box, they began to manage materials flows collaboratively with immediate suppliers, customers, and facilitating intermediaries.

Now, the focus has expanded even further as manufacturers strive to fulfill the needs of the end users of products and services while satisfying the materials supply needs of all supply chain trading partners—manufacturers' suppliers, suppliers' suppliers, distributors, tier 1 customers, tier 2 customers and so forth. For example, Hewlett-Packard Chairman and CEO Carly Fiorina has stated that the company's success following the merger with Compaq will depend on close collaboration with channel partners and on a clear understanding among vendors and solution providers of the value each adds to the supply chain.[4]

Today's leading supply chain managers have responsibilities for managing traditional functions in tandem with meeting the needs of the firm's trading partners. Progressive managers have their sights on the firm's supply chains from initial source to final end users of a company's products and services. Demand generation, demand fulfillment, and the administrative activities of channel management must be integrated and coordinated to maximize returns from supply chain activities. Business operating cycles now span the entire supply chain.

As depicted in Figure 3-1, many tissue paper manufacturers—who affectionately label their total end-end, supply chain management activities as moving toilet paper from "stump to rump"—define supply chain networks in an effort to improve efficiencies for all supply chain members. A key efficiency issue is how to compress the cycle time for moving products from the woods to the ultimate consumer. It is not unusual for the firm to spend 180 days to cycle inventories through the supply chain process from end to end.

New metrics to measure, manage, and recognize supply chain performance are being developed for trading partners to measure the efficiency and effectiveness of their supply chains. Manufacturers traditionally focused most of their strategic resources on managing internal enterprise order cycles to meet distributor needs. Now the challenge is to develop supply chains to get the firm out of the commodity/pricing game and differentiate its products and services from competition through supply chain strategic initiatives. Manufacturers are partnering with distributors to improve supply chain efficiency and the flow of materials to gain competitive advantage while improving trading partner financial returns.

Reflection Point

Am I aware of the complete supply chain for my business?
▶ In my planning do I think in terms of having a supply chain advantage or simply a product advantage?
▶ Do I think outside the "enterprise box?"

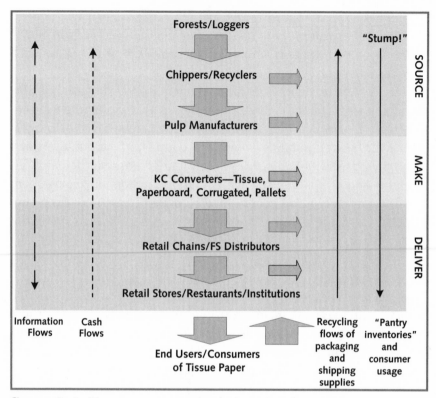

figure 3-1. Tissue paper supply chain network

Building the Business Case for Supply Chain Management

Why should a manufacturer and its distributors pursue supply chain strategic initiatives? What is the business case for investing resources—dollars, time, and systems—in supply chain network improvement?

For a $2 billion revenue manufacturer, it is not unusual that the firm and its trading partners have billions of dollars invested in inventories, accounts receivables, accounts payable, facilities, real estate, equipment for manufacturing and materials handling, customer service, and fulfillment systems performance. But is it being managed to achieve the best return and end-user retention?

Assume the above manufacturer sources direct production materials and components from 300 suppliers at 30 domestic locations. It assembles and fabricates products and components at 30 global plants, but complete assemblies can also be done at field distribution centers or at distributors. Components can then be drop-shipped directly to its 500 distributors and to end users. In analyzing the distributor network, the manufacturer found that each distributor had approximately five locations carrying an average of $1 million of the manufacturer's finished goods inventory. In addition, the end users often maintained inventories of the manufacturer's finished goods.

The point of this discussion is to identify the total dollars invested in this supply chain by all the trading partners. In this case, it was estimated that the approximate inventory investment in the supply chain approached $3 billion. For manufacturers with annual sales of $2 billion, the opportunity to reduce investment dollars of trading partners in its primary supply chain networks while improving uptime performance of its end users is dramatic. A reduction of 10 percent in the supply chain investment could result in $300 million in the profit contributions to the trading partners plus the opportunity to share some of the savings with end users by reducing prices.

Supply chain management can be critical in the healthcare industry where supplies typically represent 25 to 30 percent of a hospital's total operating expenses. For a hospital with a $1 billion annual operating budget, a disciplined supply chain initiative could decrease expenses by $20 million.[5]

To attain this level of expense reduction, several things would need to happen. First, processes (many of which are manual) would need to be streamlined and appropriate technology implemented. Second, strong and intricate relationships would need to be forged among parties across the supply chain including suppliers, payers, providers, and patients. Third, product standardization in the supply formulary would need to be examined. And finally, the system changes would need to be implemented and monitored.

The U.S. retailing industry provides another example of the value of effective supply chain management. The industry is in a continuing revolution where the goal is faster turnaround of merchandise. TAL Apparel Ltd., a closely held Hong Kong shirt maker, has developed a close relationship with JC Penney, Brooks Brothers, and Lands' End and has absorbed many supply chain functions to serve key customers.

For JC Penney, TAL collects point-of-sale data directly from the stores, decides what styles, colors, and sizes of shirts to make, and then ships them directly to each JC Penney store, bypassing the JC Penney warehouses. The result has been increased forecasting efficiency and significant decreases in inventory costs for the retailer.[6]

<table>
<tr><td rowspan="4">**Reflection Point**</td><td>**Could my firm have a better solution for end customers if I improved supply chain operations?**</td></tr>
<tr><td>▶ What resources and activities are duplicated?</td></tr>
<tr><td>▶ If these were streamlined, what would be the potential cost savings or improved efficiencies?</td></tr>
</table>

Pursuing Supply Chain Initiatives

How can you generate some quick wins in supply chain management for channel improvement? Besides doing a high-level, investment analysis of the financial accounting statements of your organization and your channel distribution partners (the macro perspective), a firm should undertake a "micro pilot" analysis to confirm the opportunities.

In moving from the macro "holistic" level to a detailed "micro" pilot level, a process team can demonstrate the return on investment (ROI) payback from investing in supply chain strategic initiatives.

Through a pilot demonstration project by a supply chain redesign team, process changes can be identified that lead to win/win benefits for manufacturers and their distributors. How are these benefits identified? The team conducts a detailed analysis of a category of the manufacturer's product/service components for selected, friendly channel members. The redesign team maps "as is" flow processes of current practices, polices, and supply chain operations.

These process maps help to identify tasks, who performs the tasks, how much time is required, and how many resources are committed to providing supply chain services. Supplier, manufacturer, distributor, and end-user processes are individually mapped and then pieced together to identify areas for improving performance. During the process, it is helpful to address the following questions:

▶ What process changes are needed?
▶ Will these changes lower costs and/or improve outcomes?
▶ What type of technology will be required to implement the process changes?

- ▶ What type of product management changes will be required?
- ▶ Is there a downside to any of the changes, and if so, what is being done to reduce the risk?
- ▶ How will accountability be handled?

This inter-enterprise, value and risk analysis leads to questions regarding why certain tasks are being performed and which, if any, can be eliminated or reduced. Areas of performance improvement are identified, such as how to reduce resource commitments, increase inventory velocity and turns, reduce cash commitments in the supply chain, reduce operating process steps, and shift or outsource responsibilities to supply chain trading partners who are better equipped to perform various tasks in the supply chain network.

Supply chain redesign runs in tandem with overall channel redesign. This microanalysis can quickly lead to "quick wins" demonstrating the ROI from investing in supply chain management. In the case of the automation control manufacturer discussed previously, the manufacturer's sales and distribution function took the lead to organize a redesign team that identified core process changes and began to work with distributors in streamlining collaborative processes, driving down inventories, improving manufacturing operations, and enhancing ultimate end-user satisfaction. This has led to increased financial returns and market share growth for the trading partners.

There are many examples of companies working toward this type of inter-enterprise process development. Goodyear, the world's largest tire company, announced in 2003 a formal supply chain management partnership with third-party logistics provider Exel. Exel will be managing more than 90 percent of the manufacturer's finished goods inventory that goes through logistics centers—about 65 million tires. To make the process work, 14 Exel employees are working closely with Goodyear to redesign its supply chain.[7]

In another example, Ford Motor Company announced in 2003 that it expects to save $350 billion as a result of its Team Value Management (TVM) supplier management initiative. By focusing on process gaps, Ford hoped to accomplish this goal with no adverse impact on suppliers' margins.[8]

For supply chain thinking to work, all trading partners must be focused upon the end user. Customer retention for future sales is key. Trading partner performance must support other supply chain member activities and recognize tradeoffs in activities and costs among the trading partners in meeting end-user demands.

The value-add contribution of trading partners must be calculated and assessed as margin impact. Information regarding stock, customer and production orders, shipments, and any diversions of stock must be available to manage material flows.

A good glossary offering information on supply chain developments is available from the Supply Chain Council. This is a nonprofit organization that has approximately 1,000 members who are working toward common definitions of supply chain processes, metrics, and enablers.[9]

Reflection Point

When pursuing channel design improvements, do I expand my thinking to include the entire supply chain?

▶ Do I start redesign from the end-user perspective?

▶ Can I identify one or two friendly distributors who would be willing to participate on an inter-enterprise team to detail what is happening in the supply chain?

▶ Am I willing to consider tradeoffs that may be more beneficial for the end user and supply chain than directly for my area of responsibility?

Supply Chain Core Processes

What can firms do to improve and redesign their supply chains? Companies can study four key processes, which are described below, in an effort to improve their supply chain operations.

Demand planning and sales forecasting. Collaborative, integrated processes composed of these major tasks provide forecasts and materials planning schedules to support the efficient flow of products and services throughout the supply chain network.

Strategic sourcing. This process involves developing strategic plans and forming alliances with suppliers to focus resources on minimizing total delivered costs and on developing new products while achieving simplified replenishment and transactional costs within the supply chain.

Manufacturing/operations strategies. This process involves obtaining maximum flexibility of production planning in using manufacturing capabilities and capacities in order to provide rapid response to changing market conditions and customer requirements.

Logistics strategies. This supply chain process plans, implements, and controls the efficient, effective flow and storage of goods, services, and related information from the point of origin to the point of consumption to meet customers' requirements.[10] This includes customer service ordering, shipment planning, transportation, warehousing, physical inventory control, packaging and unitization with reverse logistics strategies.

Key Points

▶ *Review* core supply chain processes from end-user perspectives.

▶ *Push* for strategic relationships with supply chain trading partners closest to personal and business end users and consumers. The further you are from end users, the more insulated you are from actual demand.

▶ *Cut* total supply chain cycle times.

▶ *Pursue* multi-trading partner, collaborative relationships.

▶ *Develop* relationships horizontally within a firm and vertically with trading partners—possibly including competitors!

▶ *Continue* to learn more about supply chain management and establish a company and channel supply chain steering team.

Notes

1. Ken Cottrill, "Bottom Line Leaders," *Traffic World*, 23 June 2003, p. 1.

2. *A Global Study of Supply Chain Leadership and Its Impact on Business Performance*, 2003, retrieved from www.accenture.com/xdoc/en/services/scm/scm_thought_fp.pdf.

3. "Supply Chain Challenges: Building Relationships," A conversation with Scott Beth, David N. Burt, William Copacino, Chris Gopal, Hau L. Lee, Robert Porter Lynch, and Sandra Morris, *Harvard Business Review*, July 2003, pp. 64-73.

4. Jeff O'Heir, "HP's Fiorina: Know the Value You Add," *CRN*, 14 April 2003, p. 6.

5. Lyndon Neumann, "Streamlining the Supply Chain," *Healthcare Financial Management*, July 2003, pp. 56 ff.

6. Gabriel Kahn, "Made to Measure: Invisible Supplier has Penney's Shirts all Buttoned Up," *The Wall Street Journal*, 11 September 2003, p. A1-A9.

7. Kathleen Hickey, "Let the Good Times Roll," *Traffic World*, 21 June 2003, p. 1.

8. David Hannon, "Brown Outlines Ford's Steps to Supplier Success Under TVM," *Purchasing*, 17 July 2003, p. 76.

9. Refer to www.supply-chain.org for more information. Another source is *The Supply Chain Yearbook* by John A. Woods and Edward J. Marien (McGraw-Hill, 2001).

10. Definition as published by the Council of Logistics Management (see www.clm1.org for more information).

Chapter 4

LEGAL ISSUES AND THE RESELLER CONTRACT

Legal issues might not seem as strategic as the other topics covered in the first few chapters of this book, but they can be. The forces of change discussed in the prior chapters may cause manufacturers to reexamine their downstream distribution and consequently alter business relationships.

If you understand what laws govern the relationship, you are more likely to build sound strategies. If you develop well thought out contracts, you might be able to minimize future entanglements. And you will minimize legal exposure if you request corporate counsel as you make channel changes. With advance legal analysis and advice, a channel change can be relatively painless and may even strengthen relationships with superior performers.

The intent of this chapter is to provide a brief introduction into the complex legal relationship between suppliers and their channels. The legal issues of distribution cover discriminatory practices, as well as antitrust and termination questions, and may be governed by federal laws, state laws, industry-specific laws, and/or contract terms. Because this chapter is simply an overview, please refer to *The Product Distribution Law Guide*[1]—written by lawyers in the Foley & Lardner law firm—for more detail.

The first part of this chapter will present some legal terminology relevant to the subsequent material. The second part will focus on business decisions such as market coverage, pricing, and product line policies as they relate to legal issues with the channel. The third part will discuss reasons for a written distribution agreement and thoughts on items to incorporate into it. Information on the most relevant federal laws will be woven into the discussions rather than presented as a separate section.

Terminology

Federal, state, and industry-specific laws all play a role in regulating the supplier-distributor relationship. There are both federal and state statutes focused on antitrust issues. In addition, there may be laws in all three categories that provide protection to specified distributors, dealers, franchisees, and independent sales representatives.

Antitrust laws were intended to protect trade and commerce from unlawful restraints and monopolization. These laws carry steep penalties that may include both hefty fines and jail time.

Restraints or collusive activity might occur in both vertical and horizontal relationships. Vertical relationships are those between companies at different levels in a channel of distribution (e.g., a manufacturer and a dealer). A restriction on the conduct of one of the firms in this channel by another is a *vertical restraint*. Horizontal relationships are those between two companies on the same level (e.g., two manufacturers). When these two companies agree between themselves to restrain trade (perhaps by fixing prices), it is referred to as a *horizontal restraint*.

The law most frequently associated with these issues of antitrust is the Sherman Act. Some conduct (such as horizontal price fixing) is considered automatically or *per se* illegal, regardless of the reasons for the conduct. In other situations, before a decision is made about the legality of an action, a broad assessment is made as to whether the activity was actually procompetitive. This assessment, referred to as "rule of reason," involves both parties offering economic testimony about the impact of the activity. If intrabrand competition (e.g., among distributors of the same supplier's product) is lessened without restricting interbrand competition (between competing suppliers), the activity will likely pass the rule of reason test.

Price discrimination, whereby a supplier gives channel members different prices, is governed under the Robinson-Patman Act. It is generally handled as a civil offense and rarely prosecuted on a criminal basis.

The Legal Side of Marketing Policies

There are several marketing plan components that are directly linked with channel strategy, including market coverage, pricing, and product availability. Manufacturers frequently want to control these components but should be aware of the potential legal issues related to each.

Market Coverage Decisions

There may be situations where you as a channel manager want limitations on where resellers can sell your products in order to facilitate planned market coverage. The restrictions may be in terms of geographic territories, house accounts, or industry sectors, and may be "airtight" (allowing sales only within the market area) or simply used to establish performance requirements. In any event, they should be planned with both sound business and legal consideration.

With airtight territories, distributors promise not to sell product outside their assigned territories. This *may* be viewed as a territorial restriction that is sometimes considered a vertical restraint in antitrust cases, generally governed under the Sherman Act or Section 5 of the Federal Trade Commission (FTC) Act. When challenged, this type of restriction is evaluated under the rule of reason analysis to determine whether the impact of this policy is procompetitive or anticompetitive, as discussed earlier.

Rather than use "airtight" territories, most companies prefer to define an area of primary responsibility (APR) for each distributor. When using an APR policy, suppliers require distributors to use their best efforts to meet performance requirements within the assigned territory even though they are free to sell outside the territory. Typically in this case, only sales within the APR count toward the sales quota or other performance measures. When sales are made outside the territory, suppliers should consider profit pass-over policies. With profit pass-over policies, the distributor selling outside its APR compensates the distributor in whose territory the customer is located. (Note that although the practice is widespread in the United States, territorial restrictions may not be legal in other parts of the world.)

Instead of *geographic* territory restrictions, companies may choose to limit their distributors to specific industries or customer "types," or restrict distributors from selling to "house accounts." These activities may also trigger antitrust concerns and will generally be judged by rule of reason.

Many laws and contracts were written prior to e-commerce—at a time when "territory" had a different meaning. Now suppliers, channel partners, and customers can exist everywhere and nowhere at the same time, making it more difficult to control market coverage. Therefore, the APR has become more important.

Pricing Decisions

Manufacturers develop products with specific price-value assessments in mind and are often frustrated with their inability to set prices at the user level. Although they may not *require* distributors to charge a certain price, they may *suggest* resale prices and encourage distributors in that direction. However, any tactics that are perceived as coercive (e.g., threat of termination for failure to charge a specific price) would be viewed as a violation of antitrust laws.

Questions are also raised about minimum and maximum resale price policies. When there is an agreement between a manufacturer and one or more resellers to fix a minimum price, it is per se illegal. In the past, the same was true for maximum resale price policies. However in 1997, it was determined that agreements involving maximum resale prices are to be tested against the rule of reason.[2]

Beyond price fixing, manufacturers can be challenged when they are charging different prices to different resellers. Charging different prices is not in itself illegal except in those situations as specified by the Robinson-Patman Act. A violation would need to satisfy all of the following four criteria:

1. **Two sales in interstate commerce.** Because it is quite rare for companies to deal exclusively intrastate, the requirement for interstate commerce is generally met. However, there must also be two completed sales that are relatively contemporaneous. Two *offers* to obtain product at different prices will not satisfy this criterion until both of them turn into sales.

2. **Commodities of like grade and quality.** The word *commodity* implies a physical product; therefore, service-only sales do not fall within the requirements of the Robinson-Patman Act. The prerequisite of like grade and quality may require a jury decision. In general, packaging, labeling, and branding don't necessarily constitute different products. It was determined, for example, that condensed milk was the same whether sold under private label or under the Borden label.[3]

3. **Different prices.** The price difference has to include not just the invoiced price on the product but also discounts, rebates, credits, freight waivers, and other terms that may cause the landed price to be different to customers.

4. **A hindrance to competition.** Finally, the price difference must lessen competition. This means that price differentials between customers who are *not* competing is not illegal. For example, a company selling identical goods (e.g., cars) to consumers at different prices is not illegal because the consumers are not in competition with each other.

Definitions of Competition. But competition can be on more than one level and needs to be defined. *Primary line* competition refers to injury to competition when one of two suppliers gives discriminatory prices to some customers.

For example, assume Manufacturer A gave Dealer X one price and Dealer Y a lower price. If competing Manufacturer B brought an action against A, it would be a primary line case. The claim would require proof that A's price to Y was below cost and that it created a reasonable possibility that A could drive out competition in that territory and recoup losses in the future. This is essentially a predatory pricing claim, and the antitrust risk depends partly on the market power of Manufacturer A.

A more common issue with Robinson-Patman is *secondary line* complaints—e.g., in the prior example, if X complained that Y got a better price. In that case, it would need to be proven that there was a significant difference in price or a significant difference in the time the price differential was offered. The meaning of *significant difference* is vague and would need to be determined by a jury.

It's apparent that a price differential has to satisfy several criteria before being considered a Robinson-Patman violation. And even if it is deemed a violation, a manufacturer could use one (or more) of the following defenses to justify the difference.

Defense 1: Meeting competition. A dealer may inform a manufacturer that a competing supplier (i.e., a competitor to the manufacturer) offered the dealer a lower price on a directly competitive product. The manufacturer can legally lower the price to that dealer to meet (but not beat) the competitor's price, even though this results in different prices to its dealers. Of course, there must be reasonably "good faith" in the dealer's claim of the competitive price.

Defense 2: Cost justification. A manufacturer may be able to prove that the costs of dealing with a specific reseller are lower than the costs of dealing with other resellers. However, the cost savings must equate to the price differential.

Defense 3: Functional discount. A price reduction may be given as compensation for services or tasks undertaken on behalf of the seller, e.g., providing specification activity, having a trained sales force, maintaining a showroom, participating in joint sales calls, etc.

Defense 4: Practical availability. If price discounts are based on quantities purchased, the discount steps must be *practically available* to all competing customers.

Defense 5: Changing conditions. This applies to perishable goods or those in danger of obsolescence. The manufacturer can charge lower prices to dealers buying under these conditions.

Because segmented pricing is a common marketing practice, it is worthwhile learning about the potential legal consequences of selling the same product at different prices to competing distributors.[4]

Product Line Decisions

There are two areas where product decisions within a manufacturer-distributor relationship might pose legal questions. These are exclusive dealing and tying arrangements. In both cases, rule of reason will be used to determine the impact of the actions.

Exclusive dealing is the requirement by a manufacturer that a distributor not carry competing brands. For example, Coke bottlers do not carry Pepsi products, and vice versa. Since this type of agreement "locks out" competing brands from that location, it lessens interbrand competition and may be considered an antitrust violation. However, unless the supplier has substantial power to prevent market entry into the territory by the competition (through other channel partners), there may not be substantial injury to competition.

Tying is an agreement to sell one product (i.e., the tying product) to distributors on condition that they buy a different product (i.e., the tied product). If two products are made to be used jointly, and one will not function properly without the other, tying is not illegal. Also, if each of the products can be purchased separately on the competitive market, or if the supplier lacks market power to "force" distributors to act in a way different from how they would act in a competitive environment, there will be a lower antitrust concern. The concern with tying arrangements is that manufacturers who have market power may be able to refuse to sell a popular product unless the distributor agrees to buy another product. In that case, an antitrust issue may be raised.

<table>
<tr><td>**Reflection Point**</td><td>**Do I consider the legal impact of marketing decisions on channel strategy?**
▶ Have I defined my channel's territories or markets appropriately?
▶ Have I minimized my exposure to price discrimination accusations?
▶ Am I careful in the way I structure exclusive deals and tying arrangements?</td></tr>
</table>

Written Contracts

Distributor agreements, if drafted carefully, should clarify the expectations of both parties in written form. Very often, a standard con-

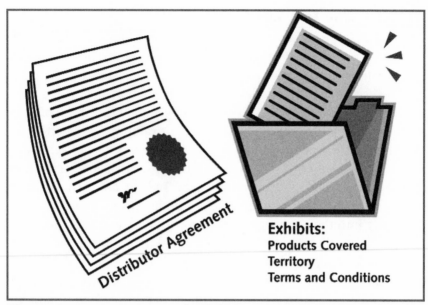

Exhibits:
Products Covered
Territory
Terms and Conditions

Distributor Agreement

Figure 4-1. Agreements and exhibits

tract covers the primary performance issues, with elements that may change from time to time addressed in separate attachments. (See Figure 4-1.)

Manufacturers (and often distributors) believe they have more flexibility without a contract, but the opposite can be true. Many statutes require "good cause" for termination, which is difficult to define without contractually specified performance.

Termination is a difficult business and personal decision that is frustrating to both parties and will result in a loss of revenue to both. A written contract can minimize your exposure to litigation by clarifying expectations.

In addition to clarifying performance standards, written contracts can achieve uniformity in the supplier-distributor relationship through the network, specify precisely how the distributor may use the supplier's trademark, and allow for future changes in the relationship (e.g., terms of sale, warranty policy, etc.). The agreement should also clarify whether the distributor is or is not a franchise, or whether the rep is or is not an agent. Typical content areas of a contract are listed in Figure 4-2.

Many suppliers choose the law of their home state to govern the

Topic	Considerations
Products	Gives the distributor the right to purchase and sell the products listed in the attached exhibit, which may be amended from time to time.
Territory	Gives the distributor the right to sell the manufacturer's products in the territory, market, or area of performance responsibility as defined in the attached exhibit, which may be amended from time to time. The manufacturer may reserve the right to add additional distributors in the territory.
Performance standards	Specifies that both parties will use their best efforts to attain the standards of performance as specified in the attached exhibit, which may be amended from time to time.
Pricing & terms	Specifies that prices are subject to change without notice.
Term of contract	Evergreen or fixed term.
Direct sales	The manufacturer retains the right to have direct sales and national accounts.
Trademark use	Describes expectations and guidelines.
Applicable law	Identifies which state law will govern the contract.
Termination	Specifies cause, timing, and benefits.
Restrictions	As appropriate for the industry and circumstances.

Figure 4-2. Typical content areas in a distributor contract

contract unless it is negative to them. However, some state laws will govern the relationship between a supplier and its distributor located in that state (or a distributor who has sales in that state), regardless of choice-of-law provisions in the contract. Legal counsel should be involved in this decision.

The contract can be written for different time frames. "Evergreen" contracts are perpetual with no specific expiration date. These are the simplest types of contracts because there is no need to review them on a specified basis. However, evergreen contracts, as compared to fixed-term agreements, are more difficult to change when market conditions change. Even if a decision is made to offer an evergreen contract, the agreement should still specify performance expectations and define causes for termination.

Fixed-term agreements allow greater ease in changing contract terms but also cause a greater administrative burden. To reduce the burden, companies may have all contracts expire on a uniform date. Companies may also choose to have a hybrid between the two—a fixed term (such as a year) with an automatic renewal for another fixed term unless the explicit decision is made to not renew.

Performance obligations for both the distributor and the manufacturer should be specified, possibly as an addendum to the contract that can be updated from time to time. Performance expectations for the distributor may include sales goals, inventory requirements, service obligations (parts availability, training, etc.), sharing of market information, forecasting, appropriate use of sub-distributors and so forth. Supplier responsibilities may include national advertising, distributor training, and promotional support. The performance obligations could detail precisely the requirements and benefits of being, for example, a premier, authorized, or affiliate distributor.

Attach an exhibit specifying the products the distributor is permitted (or not permitted) to sell. The wording should be precise enough for the manufacturer to have flexibility in future channel decisions and broad enough for distributors to be comfortable. Many companies reserve the right to use alternate channels for new products requiring specialized skills or competencies the existing distribution channel does not have or to prevent overlap if there is a merger with or acquisition of another company.

Attach the terms of sale, as well as a warranty statement, as an exhibit that can be modified from time to time at the discretion of the supplier.

The contract should contain territory provisions with an APR clause, as discussed earlier in this chapter under market coverage. The territory may be described geographically, or may specify market segments, industries, or even specific named customers. Provide an attachment listing house accounts and reserve the right to add new names to the list (either unilaterally or with distributor consent). Describe circumstances when a direct sale is permissible.

The norm for *independent rep* agreements is for them to remain in effect for an indefinite term until termination upon a reasonably short notice (30 to 90 days). Specify the criteria that entitle the rep to a commission or an order. What formula will be used to determine the commission? When is the commission payable? How will commissions be handled after termination?

With the growth of global customers and e-commerce, it becomes more difficult to define territories in a way that assures fair compensation. Agents may specify products in one territory, the actual "sale" may take place in another, and product may be shipped to yet another location. Therefore, a careful explanation of the handling of commissions is critical.

Some thought should also be given to *implementing* new contracts with existing channel members. Minor changes are generally handled through an addendum signed by both parties.

For more major changes, some negotiation may be required. First, try to make the new contract visually look as much like the old contract as possible to minimize the appearance of significant changes. Obtain copies of contracts used by supplier competitors or suppliers of complementary lines already handled by the distributor. If the suggested changes are consistent with the contracts of other companies the distributor represents, it will be an easier "sell."

If that is not possible, develop a detailed explanation of why the changes are necessary and provide a written guide for field reps to use in their discussions with distributors. Anticipate and provide answers to objections.

Reflection Point

Do I have written contracts with my channel partners?
- ▶ Do the contracts specify the performance obligations of both parties?
- ▶ Have I separated out the provisions that change into exhibits that can be periodically reviewed and updated?
- ▶ Do I have different contracts for different channel partners (e.g., premier, authorized, and affiliate distributors)?

Key Points

▶ Antitrust violations (e.g., price fixing) are per se illegal and should be avoided.

▶ Evaluate marketing decisions that may move a company into a "gray" legal area prior to implementation.

▶ Develop written contracts with your channel partners to clarify mutual expectations and minimize potential future litigation.

▶ This chapter is not legal advice. You should consult an attorney if you have any questions or concerns about the topics discussed.

Notes

1. Foley & Lardner, *Product Distribution Law Guide* (Chicago: CCH Incorporated, 1999). Information can be found at either the CCH Web site (www.cch.com) or the Foley & Lardner Web site (www.foleylardner.com).

2. Ibid, p. 9025.

3. Ibid. p. 9069.

4. In addition to the *Product Distribution Law Guide* mentioned above, two other sources provide useful explanations of price discrimination and the Robinson-Patman Act. One is *The Complete Guide to Marketing and the Law* by Robert J. Posch, Jr. (Prentice Hall, 1988). The other is *Marketing Channels*, 5th edition, by Louis W. Stern, Adel El-Ansary, and Anne T. Coughlan (Prentice Hall, 1996).

Part Two
Strategic Decisions

Chapter 5

CLARIFYING REQUIREMENTS

A Roadmap for Business Executives

As discussed in Part One, many forces are changing the face of distribution—forces that may require your company to rethink its channel design. Channel design may also need to be reevaluated during mergers or acquisitions. An initial assessment of channels to market should be part of the due diligence process on any acquisition.

All of these issues help clarify how channel planning fits with the corporate direction. The next stage of the design (as shown in Figure 5-1, next page) is defining the requirements of your channel.

Define Channel and Coverage Requirements

It's a rare company that isn't tempted to chase every opportunity that comes its way—even to the detriment of capitalizing on existing business. Philip Kotler long ago stressed target marketing, and Tom Peters preached "stick to your knitting." Chris Zook now advocates protecting your core business, and a host of other experts emphasize

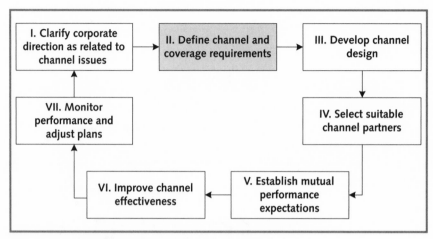

Figure 5-1. Stage II in channel redesign

the importance of a back-to-basics philosophy of growing existing customers with as much effort as (or more effort than) acquiring new customers.

Then why is it that so many managers still try to be all things to all people all of the time?

Different Customers Expect Different Things from the Channel

Start with a seemingly mundane evaluation of the current status of your firm's channel to market. As with any marketing plan, you will need to explore what end-use customers want, what the competitive dynamics are, and what the product requirements and goals of your organization are. (Note that in this first assessment the emphasis is more on end-use customers, whereas later more emphasis is placed on the needs and expectations of channel partners.) Companies routinely spend money determining *what* customers want to buy (i.e., in terms of new product development) but don't always know *how* customers want to buy (i.e., desired channels). They may know even less about how *different types* of customers want to buy.

Let's assume, for example, that your firm sells consumable office supplies such as tape, staples, paper, etc. The *usage* of these items might be quite similar across different markets, but the *buying* will be different for consumers, large businesses, and small businesses.

Consumers will generally purchase in small quantities on a cash-and-carry basis. Some small businesses will also want to buy this way, while others may prefer credit transactions, standing orders, and/or delivery. Large corporations may be looking for volume discounts and explicit delivery options. And within these markets, there may be smaller niches with more specialized needs.

The question is, what will *your* customers expect or demand from channels (both now and in the future) to be able to make a purchase decision in your favor? Here are just a few possible considerations.

- ▶ **Technical advice.** If you have a technical product, customers may expect advice on how to use it, how to make it work with existing products, how to install it, etc.
- ▶ **Product availability.** This could include sufficient inventory, ability to drop-ship, capability of fulfilling just-in-time requirements, etc.
- ▶ **Total solution.** For some customers, your product may be relatively unusable without the addition of complementary products from the distributor.
- ▶ **Supporting services.** Customers may expect installation, repair, and other services from the distributor.
- ▶ **Product customization.** Customers who require customization will prefer to deal with a reseller who can provide the requisite engineering or assembly skills.

To begin this process, identify the different end-use segments you are targeting. Then find out from them what services (and levels of each service) are important. It's insufficient to ask customers *whether*, for example, supporting services are important to them. Instead, have customers discuss *what* services are important to them and *how important* each one is.

Develop a worksheet similar to the one in Table 5-1, which presents a hypothetical information technology example. The specific services desired by three different end-customer segments—consumers, small businesses, and large businesses—are presented. Even though the segments are too broad and the example too general compared to what you will need, they are used here for illustrative purposes.

Note that in Table 5-1, consumers want technical advice, with

	Consumer	Small Business	Large Business
Technical advice	Desire hands-on demonstrations and explanations	Want ongoing support, almost as if the channel is a surrogate IT department	Limited support; handled internally by IT group
Product availability	Prefer immediate fulfillment but willing to wait	Prefer local inventory and instant availability	Prefer to have products delivered
Total solution	Want computer plus relevant ancillary products	Turn-key operation	Business plus industry-specific software and add-ons
Supporting services	Classes and CD training	Internal training and support	Training upon request; loaner products as necessary
Product customization	May be possible to provide a "fit" with existing inventory	Specific configurations preferred	Specific configurations required

Table 5-1. Hypothetical segment preferences for an IT product

hands-on demonstrations of the product. This includes advice on features appropriate for their expressed usage, along with ancillary products to be able to install and use the computer immediately. Open enrollment training or take-home CD training is perceived as a useful attribute.

The small business market, on the other hand, suggests the need for ongoing support. In fact, this market may expect the channel to serve as a "virtual" IT department, providing installation, training, upgrades, and relevant consultation on usability.

The corporate market is looking for larger volume, customized fulfillment, and—most likely—products specified by their internal IT departments. For ancillaries and supplies, these customers may want to monitor contract versus off-contract purchasing, branded versus private label buying, and to have access to reports on cost savings. Manufacturers going after these markets need to find channels providing the most relevant services.

Once the customer expectations and requirements have been

identified, it is useful to map them against the various channels to decide where the match is best. All of these differing expectations cannot be fully met by one channel.

Develop a grid similar to Table 5-2 for *each identified market*. This particular grid evaluates which channels offer each of the services expected of the small business market. The checks indicate your assessment of the best channel for providing the indicated activities. The value-added resellers and specialty distributors appear to offer the best "fit" to supply the services expected by this specific end-use market. Similar grids for other markets may suggest different channels.

In the previous example, customers were defined primarily by

	Consumer Preferences (from prior table)	Retail	VAR	Specialty Distributor Wholesaler	Internet	Direct Sales Force
Technical advice	Desire hands-on demonstrations and explanations		✔	✔		✔
Product availability	Prefer immediate fulfillment but willing to wait			✔	✔	
Total solution	Want computer plus relevant ancillary products	✔		✔		
Supporting services	Classes and CD training		✔			✔
Product customization	May be possible to provide a "fit" with existing inventory		✔		✔	✔

Table 5-2. Small business market channel grid

size of purchase, but other approaches can be used. There may be differences between residential versus commercial, vertical industry A versus vertical industry B, or geography X versus geography Y customers. The clearer the boundaries between customer groups, the easier it will be to design different channel structures to reach them.

Channel Preferences Are Not Static

In studying customer channel preferences, look at both behavior (what channels they buy from now) and preferences (what channels and channel services they would like in the future). Ask customers what channels they would *like* to buy from, what channels they might *consider* buying from and what channels they would *never* buy from.

Provide categories such as independent rep, catalog distributor, specialty distributor, big box retailer, Internet, and/or any other categories relevant to your industry. It is worth noting that the distinction between channel types is blurring as reps begin to stock products and distributors drop-ship, but it is a useful starting point.

Be sure to collect demographic data such as age, sex, income, and location, or "firmographic" data such as customer type and size, transaction volume, and functional title to look for segments that may have different needs.[1] Also, encourage open discussion on the problems or difficulties customers have experienced with various channel types (not specific firms) and any suggestions they might have for improvements.

Different circumstances may promote channel shifting. Downsizing may shift priorities from price to service as customers need more support from the channel to replace the internal support lost. Unexpected urgency for a product may cause customers to forego existing loyalties to purchase from a channel with the product in stock, rather than wait for a back order.

Volvo provides an example of adapting channel functions to respond to different circumstances. Between 1993 and 1995, Volvo GM Heavy Truck Corporation's dealers began to report stock-outs on critical parts. Upon careful analysis, Volvo GM determined that dealers were able to predict parts requirements for scheduled maintenance quite well. However, emergency roadside repair was a quite different situation. Because demand could not be predicted and dealers were unwilling to carry every part all the time, there were stock-outs.

To deal with this situation, Volvo set up a warehouse that would stock the full line of truck parts and contracted with FedEx Logistics to provide immediate delivery for emergency repairs. This resulted in better supply chain management of inventory. Dealer revenues went up, and Volvo was able to eliminate three warehouses.[2]

Buying behavior also changes over time. As people become more comfortable with a product or service, they become more self-sufficient. Priorities shift from service and training to ease of doing business and lower prices. It is at this point that companies need to consider streamlining the channel (and providing customers what they want), rather than adding unnecessary value-added services (and pushing on to customers what they don't want).

This isn't meant to imply that companies should resort to discounting and price wars but, rather, that firms should consider these channel shifts as part of a larger strategy also involving new product development and other efforts.

Industry and Competition

Once you have determined what your targeted end-customers want and expect in terms of channel performance, you must also evaluate the channels that competitors use to go to market. Have competitors (who in the past used traditional distributors) added big box retailers to their mix? Has there been a shift from specialty distributors to catalog distributors? Have nontraditional channels gained prominence? What has been the cause of these shifts?

If distributors are selling to dealers or retailers, it's important to understand that relationship. Just-in-time inventory can be very important for independent retailers who don't have large warehouses because it helps them compete with the big boxes. A manufacturer involved in two-step distribution to such a market would need to specify this capability as a channel requirement.

Similarly, some dealers and retailers have come to rely on and expect true supply chain management and logistics services from their distributors. Brightpoint, for example, an Indianapolis-based distributor that services big box consumer electronics chains, packages equipment manufacturer bulk accessories into retailer-specific packages. Navarre Distribution Services in Minneapolis applies price and rebate stickers on products for specific customers and maintains a vendor-managed inventory system to provide category management for retailers. D&H Distributing in Harrisburg, Pennsylvania, has six distribution centers across the country; these locations allow the company to brand and drop-ship from coast to coast. Their customers can place and trace orders via the D&H Web site.[3]

The financial services industry has also gone through changes that may impact channel requirements. Grange Mutual Insurance and State Farm Insurance, for example, have both opened banks to expand financial and insurance offerings and market accessibility to their customers. Bank of America has more than 1,000 financial advisers, 95 percent of whom are licensed to sell life insurance.[4] Both the financial services and insurance companies are adapting to changing channel requirements in these industries.

High tech companies in industries such as electronics, chemicals, and pharmaceuticals outsource production to contract manufacturers and expect distributors to provide supply chain solutions. Expected activities include "inventory management, bonded and consignment inventory programs, parts flow control, logistics management, and assorted supplier research and management input."[5] The face of this industry and the actions of the competing companies in it will influence what is expected in terms of channel performance.

Product Requirements Influence Channel Selection

In addition to evaluating customer and competitive issues in channel design, you must also consider the needs of your product. In general, more complex products are "high-touch," meaning they require more human contact and service. Off-the-shelf, standard products are "low-touch," requiring less human interaction. The types of channels that are high-touch versus low-touch, along with a categorization by direct and indirect, are shown in Figure 5-2.

The high-touch, direct channels include your own sales force and company-owned resellers (both domestic and foreign). Within this group you can exert significant control in terms of training, performance measures, and brand equity. The low-touch, direct channels include the corporate Website, telesales, and direct mail. Although you maintain control, there is less two-way dialog with customers.

The high-touch, indirect channels include manufacturer's reps, specialty distributors, value-added resellers and brokers/jobbers. The individuals in these channels generally have strong industry knowledge and good customer connections but necessarily operate in the best interest of their firm rather than yours. The low-touch, indirect channels, including catalog distributors, mass retailers and third party Web sites, offer the advantage of reach and (at least with

	High-Touch	Low-Touch
Direct	**Sales Force Company-Owned Resellers Foreign Direct Investment**	**Corporate Web Site Telesales Direct Mail**
Indirect	**Manufacturer's Rep Force Specialty Distributor Value-Added Reseller Brokers, Jobbers, etc.**	**Catalog Distributor Mass Retailer Third-Party Internet Site**

Figure 5-2. Channel types by service requirement

the first two) local inventory.

Friedman and Furey, in their book *The Channel Advantage*,[6] present the following nine attributes as indicators of appropriate product-channel fit.

1. **Definition:** the extent to which a product is easily known and recognized. Most mature, packaged, consumer products fit here. The clearer the definition, the easier it is to use low-touch and indirect channels.

2. **Customization:** the amount of product adaptation required by customers. This can vary from offering a product with different options to offering totally customized products. The more customization required, the better the fit with high-touch channels.

3. **Aggregation:** whether the product is a stand-alone solution. In computers, for example, hardware requires software to run and is therefore not a complete solution without it. If a product must be "bundled" with complementary products from another firm to provide a total solution to customers, indirect channels will probably be required.

4. **Exclusivity:** the uniqueness of an offering. Part of the aura of uniqueness comes from reduced availability. Products that are perceived as unique will generally do better with direct channels, or selective high-touch indirect channels.

5. **Customer education:** the need for knowledge during and after the sale. Many highly complex products may have benefits that are not readily apparent. The more education required by customers, the greater the need for high-touch channels.

5. **Substitution:** the ease with which a product can be replaced by a competing offering. The more substitutable a product, the more a company will want to exert "control" with a direct channel. On the other hand, if customers are not willing to go out of their way to buy a particular brand, mass channels may be necessary to stay within reach.

6. **Maturity:** the stage of a product in a life cycle. New-to-the-world products may be less defined and require more customer education, suggesting a greater desire for high-touch channels. As products move toward commodity status, low-touch and/or indirect channels become appropriate.

7. **Customer risk:** refers to the potential consequences (business, personal, health, etc) of a wrong decision. For example, getting the wrong or insufficient insurance coverage can be damaging at the time of a claim. The greater the risk, the more likely a high-touch channel will be desired.

8. **Negotiation:** the degree to which the scale or complexity of a sale prevents a simple transaction. This is the case with bid situations, where engineering approaches and/or various services can be adapted for unique circumstances. Product sales requiring negotiation lean toward high-touch channels.

In most traditional situations, channels were thought of as offering complete "packages"—manufacturers chose distributors, dealers, reps, etc., that provided most of the desired services in the package. Recently, companies have begun to disaggregate the channel functions and activities to better understand the value provided. By analyzing the required activities and the costs of providing the activities, manufacturers can better create the appropriate channel to satisfy customer needs.

Understanding product requirements will help assess the viability of various channel types. But it is also important to consider a firm's short- and long-term vision. Does the company have a goal of penetrating new markets, entering foreign countries, or consolidating channels after a merger? What is the targeted sales revenue for the products and services of interest? What will be the territorial coverage requirements to satisfy these goals?

Efficient Territorial Coverage Must Be Sought

Determining coverage is at best an inexact science. A company must decide whether it wants to have regional, national, or international coverage; whether the product requires intensive or controlled (selective) distribution to be effective; and what its financial goals are. As these decisions are being made, there will necessarily be tradeoffs (unless there are absolutely no time, resource, or budget constraints!).

To reach a given market share goal it may be necessary to have more intensive distribution than would be preferred from a strictly product perspective. To gain quick vertical market growth, it may be necessary to have more specialized distribution than would otherwise be preferred.

Some trade associations provide estimates of market potential, possibly even by trading area. A trading area can be defined as a ZIP code, a city, a county, a state, or any combination of these, including potentially the surrounding dependent area. *Agency Sales* magazine (the publication of the Manufacturers' Agents National Association or MANA), for example, has divided the United States into 28 standard trading areas (along with some international trading areas). Their directory of reps (as discussed in Chapter 8) uses these standard trading areas for search and placement purposes.

The generic trading area designation is a starting point. Get input from your own sales force to determine whether specific trading areas are larger or smaller for your needs. Once the size of the trading areas is refined, estimate market potential from customer surveys (on what they buy), distributor input, industry approximations, or census statistics on the number of companies in a given industry classification or on total consumer population (see www.census.gov for descriptions of data sources and uses). Then compare your current sales with the potential to calculate your market share. If the share is less than expected for any territory, it may be due to one or more of several factors including product fit, distribution availability, and win rate.[7]

Product fit refers to the percent of the total market your product or service "fits." For example, if your product is relevant only to a specific niche within the overall market or if there are significant gaps in your product line, your offering will not be appropriate for the entire market.

Distribution availability refers to the percent of opportunities where your product is present. If your product were in every relevant channel type and presented through every intermediary, the availability would be 100 percent. Finally, the win rate refers to how often your product wins the sale—the win/loss ratio.

In a situation where your product is relevant to 60 percent of the overall market (product fit), is available in 80 percent of the potential outlets serving the market (distribution availability), and you win the sale 30 percent of the time (win rate), your market share is 14 percent, as shown below.

Market share = product fit x distribution availability x win rate

14 percent = 60 percent x 80 percent x 30 percent

To improve these numbers you must decompose the figures. Product fit can be improved through better product development, a more complete product line, and/or improved communications with customers. Distribution availability can be improved by adding distributors who focus on the correct group of end customers. Win rate can be improved by providing your channel with better support, expanding the corporate brand and marketing efforts, ensuring the appropriate price point, and/or guaranteeing the appropriate solutions for customers.

In the example above, the weakest number (at 30 percent) is the win rate, so primary emphasis should be placed on improving that value. Is the product perceived as weaker than the competition? Would better sales training increase the win rate?

Reflection Point

How effective is my channel's territorial coverage?
▶ Do I have enough of the right products for the targeted customers?
▶ Are my products offered at enough locations and at the right locations for my customers?
▶ How often do my channel partners present my product to their customers as an option for satisfying their needs?

Develop Channel Design

After gaining an understanding of channel and coverage requirements in Stage II, you can begin to evaluate your existing channel
and then either improve the performance of the current channel
and/or work toward a new channel strategy. To improve the existing
channel, you may choose to recruit new distributors to fill gaps in
specific territories, drop some non-growable distributors, and work
with other distributors to help them become better businesses.

It is unlikely that one channel will address all of the needs of even
one targeted segment (as was shown earlier). In addition, your
products may require different channel services than may seem
appropriate for defined target markets. Statistics from a trade association in the insurance industry, for example, reveal that the average
number of distribution channels a life insurance company supports
today is four.[8]

So your job is to either (a) look for a "best match," (b) choose
multiple channels to allow flexibility in satisfying specific needs,
and/or (c) build your own "hybrid" channel by supplementing services from different sources as necessary.

Start by defining the primary products and markets impacting
the channel decision. Let's expand the prior IT example to include
off-the-shelf products, customized products, and ancillary products
for the three market segments of consumers, small business, and
large business. This is shown in Figure 5-3.

Off-the-shelf products are not customized and are more mature
and well defined than the others, lending themselves to low-touch.
Customized products require more negotiation and education, lending themselves to high-touch channels. However, given the financial
reality of the consumer market, a direct sales force would be inappropriate and would need to be replaced with either a low-touch
direct or a high-touch indirect channel.

Ancillary products are not stand-alone solutions and therefore lend
themselves to indirect channels—particularly if they are "generic." On
the other hand, if the quantity is large enough and built into a customized sale, high-touch channels become appropriate.

Note that there is an interaction between product requirements
and customer needs, resulting in specific product-markets that are

Products Markets	Off-the- shelf	Customized	Ancillary Products
Consumers	Low- Touch Channels	Low-Touch Direct or High- Touch Indirect	Indirect Channels
Small Business		High-Touch	
Large Business			

Figure 5-3. Product-market channel grid

best served by different channel types. Office supplies distributors understand the differing needs of large customers for the primarily commodity products they carry.

Boise Office Solutions maintains "Customer Insight Reports" that detail purchase behavior of multiple location customers to help the corporate purchasing department monitor user compliance to national agreements. Staples began testing a "no returns" program in spring 2003 with five customers. Under the program, customers donate items to charity rather than return them and are issued a credit. The intent of the program is to streamline internal processes, thereby lowering costs.[9] In both of these cases, manufacturers have to work closely with the channel to address specific product-market needs.

Management will need to make a decision on which options to pursue and on the best way(s) to proceed. Once that decision is made, the next issue is to determine the number of distributors or channel partners to work with. Start by estimating the total revenue opportunity for each product market and determine a realistic sales benchmark per distributor. Then divide the revenue opportunity by the sales benchmark to provide an approximate number of distributors.

If this figure suggests you have a sufficient number of distributors, look at the territory analysis described earlier to determine whether you have appropriate coverage where you need it. You may need to increase the number of distributors in certain territories and/or improve their productivity.

In addition, you will need to look at the product-market sales and servicing requirements to determine whether the existing distributors can handle them or whether distinct service partners will be necessary. Chances are that multiple channels will be necessary to attain financial goals. Chapters 6 and 7 explore these issues in more depth. The goal is to determine the right channel(s) for each product-market, the right number of partners in each channel, and the best tools to improve channel performance.

Channel conflict is bound to occur whenever there are multiple channels to market. Not all conflict is bad—and can even be positive for the manufacturer when out-of-date or uneconomic players are forced to adapt or improve. However, a minimization of conflict, when possible, is generally one of the goals of a good channel design.

Select Suitable Channel Partners

By now, you have decided on the best channel type(s) given the needs of your target customers, your products, and your internal goals. You have determined in which trading areas you need to add channel members or change the channel structure while minimizing unnecessary conflict. And you have compiled a list of candidates satisfying the requirements.

The most suitable channel partners will have a business model consistent with your goals and channel requirements as described in this chapter. Chapter 8 describes the search methodology and process for negotiating the best channel agreement. Chapter 9 helps in the negotiation process by clarifying differences in perspectives between manufacturers and distributors.

Establish Mutual Performance Expectations

The identification of the ideal channel and selection of candidates that embody that ideal go a long way to establish the "right" channel design. However, motivation and management will always be necessary to ensure continued successful results.

Also, conditions change over time, and the support and monitoring of the channel will need to be flexible during those changes. Part Three of this book focuses on managing the ongoing relationships within the channel. Chapter 10, in particular, stresses the importance of setting mutual expectations. Several measures may be used to measure performance, including the following:

- ▶ sales volume
- ▶ percent sales to target customers
- ▶ sales growth rate
- ▶ operating margins
- ▶ inventory turnover
- ▶ average inventory
- ▶ percent sales from stock
- ▶ sales calls per month
- ▶ attainment of sales quota
- ▶ market share
- ▶ actual-to-planned sales
- ▶ company complaints
- ▶ inventory maintained
- ▶ customer satisfaction
- ▶ gross margin return on inventory investment (GMROI)

The final measure, GMROI, combines margin management and inventory management. It allows the distributor or dealer to evaluate inventory on its investment return rather than using a simple gross margin percentage.

Improve Channel Effectiveness

Chapter 11 overviews the many types of programs manufacturers might provide to channel partners to motivate and improve performance. Some are short-term (such as contests for a new product launch), while others are ongoing (such as co-op advertising programs). As a starting point, it is useful to compare your planned support programs with the competition and determine who offers the channel "best-in-class" programs using a format such as shown in Figure 5-4.

Develop metrics to evaluate the effectiveness of programs. Look for more than the percentage of partners using the program. Think

Program	Company			Best-in-Class
	A	B	C	

Marketing Communications
  Pass-through
    materials
  Shelf displays
  Web templates
	○
	○
	●
		○
		●
		○
			○
			●
			○
				B: creates custom
				  newsletters
				C: provides interactive tool
				A: simple inserts

Coop Funding	1-7%	1-2%	2-4%	

Lead Referral
  Web hotlink
  Prospect database
  Direct mail leads
	●
	—
	○
		—
		●
		○
			—
			●
			○
				A: shopping cart to partner
				C: online access to
				  prospects
				C: prioritizes leads

Event Marketing
  Trade shows
  Industry events
	●
	—
		●
		●
			●
			●
				A: cosponsors at no
				  additional cost
				B: organizes industry
				  events

Sales Support
  Joint sales calls
  Sales training
  Collateral material
	○
	●
	○/●
		○
		●
		○/●
			●
			●
			○/●
				A: makes more joint calls
				  than others
				B: provides flexible
				  training
				A: $175 free each quarter

Key: ○ = Available free   ● = Available for a fee   — = Not available

Figure 5-4. Competitive support programs

about the outcomes you would like to justify your expenditure in channel programs and develop metrics based on those outcomes.

Monitor Performance and Adjust Plans

The last stage of the process is auditing the channel and making adjustments as necessary. Part of the auditing process will occur informally as part of the ongoing monitoring, but it may be useful to augment this with formal surveys, distributor advisory councils, and periodic distributor evaluations (see Chapter 12). Part of the distributor evaluations will involve determining a particular distributor's "growability."[10]

Distributors (like any business) can be divided into self-growing, growable, and nongrowable. *Self-growing distributors* are strong businesspeople with a desire to develop their firms for the future and who have put plans in place to make it happen. Generally, these are the types of distributors who will grow with or without your help.

Growables are those distributors who have a desire to grow their business but could benefit from help from their suppliers. *Nongrowables* are those distributors who are comfortable with their current situation and have a status quo orientation.

Suppliers will sometimes misallocate their support across these types of distributors. Because we generally want to turn around the bad performance of the nongrowables, we spend inordinate time and effort providing support. And because we generally enjoy and appreciate the self-growing distributors, we reward them with additional funds and support—even though they would be successful without them. That leaves very little time and money left for the growables—the group of distributors who could really benefit from your support (as shown by the dotted line in Figure 5-5). To the extent possible, manufacturers should attempt to reduce their support of the two extremes to allow more support of the growables.

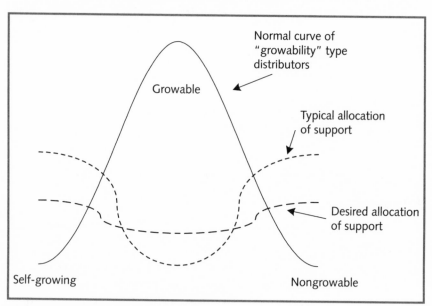

Figure 5-5. Distributor growability

Part of the audit should include how well you are performing as a supplier. Some of this information will come out of the distributor advisory council. However, a comparative survey in which distributors compare your performance to their other suppliers can be enlightening. Figure 5-6 (page 88) shows an example survey adapted from one that a manufacturer used to solicit input from its channel.

Key Points

▶ Defining channel requirements should start with an examination of the expectations of the different priority end-customers, sales requirements of different products, and the resulting product/market requirements.

▶ Territorial coverage evaluations should consider product fit, distribution availability, and win rate.

▶ Channel design may go beyond traditional structures to include different channels to different product markets and/or partnering with nontraditional companies to provide select services.

▶ Recruiting the *right* partners is more effective than attempting to change the *wrong* partners.

▶ Compare your support programs with those of the competition and analyze "best-in-class."

▶ Use the growability scale, the satisfaction survey, and advisory councils to improve the support you provide to channels.

Notes

1. Although now out of print, *Segmentation Marketing* by John Berrigan and Carl Finkbeiner (New York: HarperBusiness, 1992) provided an interesting discussion on profiling and understanding business-to-business market segments. For consumer markets, *Segmentation and Positioning for Strategic Marketing Decisions* by James Myers (Chicago: American Marketing Association, 1996) offers a more statistical and psychographic perspective on segmentation. Many firms with good customer relationship management systems would also be able to perform this type of analysis.

2. James A. Narus and James C. Anderson, "Rethinking Distribution," *Harvard Business Review*, July-August 1996, pp. 112-120.

3. Alan Wolf, "Distributors Playing a Larger Role in Retail Operations," *Twice*, 24 March 2003, pp. 20-22.

Instructions:

a. Review each issue and rate its importance (Column 3) from 1-5, with 1 = low and 5 = high.

b. Select two other suppliers and list their names below "competitive supplier."

c. Rate us and the two identified suppliers in terms of performance on the identified issue, using a 1-5 scale, with 1 = low and 5 = high.

Issue	Description	Importance (from 1-5)	Supplier Rating (from 1-5)			Comments
			Our Firm	Competitive Supplier	Competitive Supplier	
Product Innovation	True improvements; not just "me too" products					
Product availability	Delivered on time					
	Minimal backorders					
	Accurate shipments					
Responsive-ness	Quick response to inquiries					
Product knowledge	Supplier employees have thorough product knowledge					
Support	Returns handled fairly					
	Effective warranty resolution					
	Quality distributor training					
	Effective promotional support					
	Joint sales calls					
	Fair return policies					
Ease of doing business	Easy order checking					
	Accessibility to staff					
Pricing	Consistent pricing					
	Fair margins					
Overall						

Figure 5-6. Example distributor satisfaction survey

4. Lee Ann Gjertsen, "B of A Insurance-Sales Play: Commercial-Free," *American Banker*, 11 August 2001, p. 1.

5. James P. Morgan, "Distributors, CMs Find a Place in the Supply Chain," *Purchasing*, 6 March 2003, Vol. 132, No. 4, p. 25.

6. Lawrence G. Friedman and Timothy R. Furey, *The Channel Advantage* (London, England: Butterworth-Heinemann, 1999). Chapter 4 provides a more thorough discussion of product-channel fit.

7. The discussion on the channel's impact on market share was adapted from information from the consultancy, Frank Lynn & Associates (www.franklynn.com).

8. Barry Higgins, "Advanced Sales Areas Face Challenge of Quantifying Efforts," *National Underwriter*, 2 December 2002, p. 44.

9. Anonymous, "Need Help Managing Costs? Distributors Can Lend Hand," *Purchasing*, 15 May 2003, pp 57-59.

10. Adapted from Frank Lynn & Associates, see Note 7.

Chapter 6

CHANNEL DESIGN

After reviewing the many forces and strategic factors leading to channel selection, the question is: what are some analytical techniques and key enablers to implementing channel redesign? As originally presented in Chapter 1, Figure 6-1 represents a methodical, staged approach to investigating the present status of your organization leading to redesigned channel strategies and business plans.

Companies are continually testing and refining their approaches. Now you have to use information previously presented to build channels by (a) tweaking your existing channel to improve corporate position, (b) choosing multiple channels to allow flexibility in satisfying segmented end-user and customer needs, and (c) building hybrid channels by contracting or outsourcing different services as necessary to more effectively meet the same or different end-user needs.

The purpose of this chapter is to focus on Stage III of this change management process for developing and implementing channels to achieve the organizational goals and strategic initiatives discussed in Part One. Later chapters will address the rollout and implementation of strategy in relation to targeted channel and channel member selections.

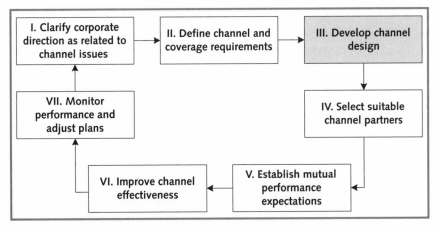

Figure 6-1. Stage III of channel redesign

Revisiting Channel Goals

Even though corporate goals were evaluated during the first stage of channel design or refinement, it is useful to periodically return to these "big picture" goals to ensure that any channel modifications are consistent with the direction of the company. Ask yourself whether your channel design is the most effective and efficient approach to attain revenue/profit targets, achieve product and market objectives, grow internationally (if that is a corporate directive), and implement your marketing plan.

Let's consider an example of a manufacturer of medical equipment who supplies hospital and clinic laboratories with whole goods as well as service parts. A key strategic goal is to get closer to the patient and clinic operations in order to make laboratories more profitable and productive with less downtime. Many manufacturers in this industry are installing electronic monitoring systems with communications connections back to field service centers to remotely monitor equipment operations. At the same time, these manufacturers are working with laboratories on patient management systems to schedule usage.

As usage and equipment functionality is monitored, more sophisticated preventive maintenance procedures are ensuring equipment up time and improving equipment/operator productivity. Thus, manufacturers are establishing channels to get closer to patients and operators to determine the real usage instead of relying on break-down information and second-hand usage reporting.

If distributors are involved in the channel, second- and third-hand information can create unreliable replenishment data and, consequently, inventory slush. As medical equipment manufacturers get closer to end users, forecasting takes on more collaborative functionality as opposed to the separate forecasting and scheduling systems by trading partners that rely on traditional purchasing and inventory control processes.

Globalization efforts can also impact channel strategy. A company with a goal of expanding globally should define the rollout strategy—country by country—to prioritize its go-to-market efforts. Then the channel design should be consistent with these efforts. Unfortunately, what commonly happens is a more random process whereby the manufacturer obtains an order from a distributor or agent in another country and begins its international distribution with that purchase order.

Regardless of the type of channel change that may be required, the execution will be more acceptable if the manufacturer is perceived as having integrity and has taken the time to develop trust with channel partners. Figure 6-2 contains a self-evaluation template for a manufacturer to use to judge its trust level and to identify ways to improve it.

Several people should probably complete the template to look for opportunities that may be missed by one person. The first column contains nine factors that relate to perceived trust; the second column is to be used to rate your performance on each factor; and the final column contains space for you to write steps or recommendations for improvement.

Reflection Point

What are my company's major strategic goals?
▶ Can the goals be accomplished with the existing channel structure?
▶ Have I prioritized new target markets (or countries) in terms of my channel structure?

Factor	Rating (1-5)	Indicate what you can do to improve the rating
Integrity: are you perceived as a company that stands behind its promises?		
Two-way communication: do you consistently share information with channel partners and listen to their feedback?		
Fairness: do you treat all channel partners equitably, and is there a realistic appeals process for concerns?		
Consistency: do you maintain consistency in your policies and procedures?		
Knowledge: do you demonstrate knowledge about your industry and the markets?		
Respect: do you show respect for your channel partners?		
Interdependence: are you willing to relinquish some of your independence to work with channel partners?		
Empathy: do you understand the world of your distributors and dealers and have their interests at heart?		
Competence: do your channel partners believe you can deliver?		

Figure 6-2. Assessing trust

Instructions: Rate your company on each of the following nine factors to assess the perceived trust level among channel members, then develop steps you might take to improve the rating.

Renovating Existing Channels

Companies should not switch to different channel structures without careful consideration. Sometimes the existing channel design is basically sound and simply requires some tweaking to be able to fit corporate and strategic goals and/or address customer requirements. Even when big customers ask for a direct sales channel, the ability of the manufacturer to handle all services related to the direct sale should be evaluated. Changing the channel may incur channel conflict without improving service to the end customer.

Caterpillar has publicly stated that its system of distribution and product support gives it a significant competitive advantage. Its management realizes that the local dealers are established members of their communities and, as such, have strong links with the end customers. They provide a wide range of services before, during, and after the sale of Caterpillar products—services that could not be provided as effectively by the manufacturer. In fact, two of the criteria the firm uses in evaluating potential new products are whether they will fit the current distribution system and whether the distribution system will add value to the product.[1]

Several high-tech companies, such as IBM, Microsoft, and Cisco, have also realized the value of their value-added resellers (VARs) and have policies (as of 2002) to minimize conflicts. In IBM's case, their software reps cannot take a direct customer order without getting management approval and are expected to work with the local channel partner in the deal.

Microsoft urges its sales staff to work with the channel partners and provides the partners with commissions on the product or license sales by its direct (internal) staff. Cisco ties sales force compensation to partner involvement, providing credit to its direct sales force only for products sold to customers through solutions providers.[2] In all of these cases, the manufacturers deemed their existing channel structures as being most appropriate for their long-term goals, and developed policies to protect existing channel members.

The renovation of existing channels may include restructuring programs and modifying strategies to motivate distributors, reps, and dealers to higher performance and/or leverage the strength of the channel while compensating for the weaknesses. As an example of restructuring programs, manufacturers have begun to shift away from volume discounting toward activity-based compensation to reward channel partners for performing value-added functions that make the channel more efficient. These functions can include having product specialists on staff, providing supplier-managed inventory services, training customers, or maintaining showrooms. Microsoft, for example, proposed a new compensation system in the mid-1990s to provide a set fee per service call to encourage its solution providers to profitably provide service to the end customers.[3] In this situation, the primary tactical objectives are to improve the working relationship with channel partners.

To begin this process, it may be useful to clarify what each channel partner does best (or worst). Start by examining whether functions could be shifted among channel partners to improve overall channel efficiency. Table 6-1 (page 96) provides a worksheet to use to prioritize cost and evaluate how well each channel partner provides the indicated functionalities.

Of course, as the number of channel partners increases, the ability to shift functions can become cumbersome. Hewlett-Packard's Small/Medium Business (SMB) Organization had more than 20,000 channel partners selling everything from pocket calculators to computer networks. To manage the interactions, the company established a partner relationship management (PRM) program—similar to a customer relationship management (CRM) program—that leverages technology to build value into the relationship.[4] Other companies provide categories of resellers, such as premier, authorized, and affiliate distributors. Although manufacturers use these different distributor "levels" in an attempt to improve channel relations, any time there is an ability and desire to grab business from another channel member, there can be conflict in the channel.

Conflict Within an Existing Channel

As mentioned in the preceding section, manufacturers attempt to reduce conflict within their existing channel by establishing specific performance requirements to earn special compensation and prices. For example, a premier distributor may be expected to share market analysis data, have an outside sales force and create account plans,

Functional Responsibilities (who does what?)	Manufacturer	Intermediary/ Facilitator	Distributor	Dealer/ Contractor	End User
Product Design					
Marketing					
Promotions					
Sales					
Customer Service/Order Entry					
Field Service Support					
Importing					
Quality Assurance					
Inventory Management					
Manufacturing/Converting					
Manufacturing/Operations					
Transportation					
Warehousing					
Exporting					
Invoicing and Billing					
Credit and Collections					
Returns					
IT/Data Warehousing					
Human Resources					
Strategic Planning					
Supply Chain Planning					
Capital Financing					

Table 6-1. Channel partner value assessment: worksheet to analyze member functionality

maintain specific inventory, and provide a complete service and repair function—in exchange for preferred pricing and product availability.

An authorized distributor may be expected to share market analysis data, have a telemarketing operation, and maintain specific inventory. An affiliate distributor may have access to the manufacturer's products without being given any special pricing or compensation.

When there are too many distributors in a given area, or when one distributor "cherry-picks" accounts in another distributor's territory, there can be price competition and conflict. Suppliers attempt to reduce some of the conflict by establishing either exclusive (airtight) territories or areas of primary responsibility (APR). The use of exclusive territories should be discussed with legal counsel to be sure there are no potential antitrust violations. When distributors are assigned an APR, there is generally an expectation that a specific sales volume (quota) must be attained within the stated boundaries (either geographic or customer/industry-based). Sales into another distributor's territory might not be credited toward the quota, or there might be a "profit pass-over" policy where some of the profit is shared with the affected distributors.

A final area where conflict may arise is when some existing channel partners are not the right ones for execution of your strategy and for addressing customer needs. This may be the result of a split in direction between your strategy and the distributor's strategy, or it may be that the initial selection was inappropriate. In either case, conflict will be present. In this case, the manufacturer must decide whether the specific channel partner can and will make changes consistent with your direction, or whether it is better to part ways.

Reflection Point

Have I carefully evaluated my current channel structure to look for areas of improvement?

▶ Can improvements be made by shifting functions to different channel partners and compensating them appropriately?

▶ Are steps taken to maintain trust during any changes and to minimize conflict among channel partners?

Managing Multiple Channels

Fewer and fewer companies use a single channel structure to reach their markets. When there are several market segments with different needs, or distinctly different product markets, it may be necessary to reach them with different channels. Companies must explore whether their customers or corporate goals dictate a direct or indirect channel, one- or two-step distribution, specialist or generalist intermediaries, a nontraditional approach to market, or some combination of these approaches.

And the choices are enormous. Lehman Brothers, a global financial consulting company, indicates that there are more than 300,000 U.S. distributors, most of which are privately held with less than $25

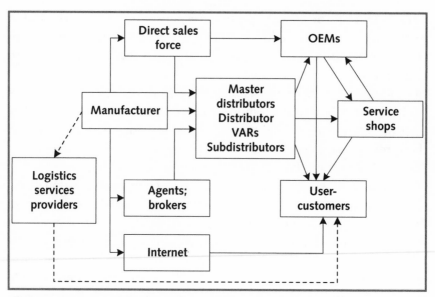

Figure 6-3. Simplified multiple channel structure

million in revenues. There are only 120 publicly traded distributors, and they are concentrated in (a) food, grocery, and retail products; (b) technology products; and (c) healthcare products.[5] A relatively simple channel structure with multiple approaches to the end customer is shown in Figure 6-3.

Each approach has potential advantages and disadvantages. Direct channels may establish stronger connections with end customers but may be cost-prohibitive or not supply the complete solution customers are seeking. Indirect channels may enable one-stop shopping for customers but may be perceived as added expense. Companies that deal with multiple channels strive to find the best match with channel capabilities and customer needs and then develop plans for reducing potential conflict.

Conflict with the Manufacturer over a New Channel

Conflict can occur when there are house accounts, national accounts, or other situations where a manufacturer wants to maintain control. Channel members fear the loss of current income and the potential for the manufacturer to squeeze them out of future business. Both are reasonable concerns.

To minimize conflict, the manufacturer should specify its right to house accounts (under specific conditions) in the initial distributor contract (see Chapter 4). This should spell out a fair process for both the supplier and channel member to avoid destroying the trust that should have been built up by this time. Reps, in particular, are paranoid that a principal will take a rep's business and turn it over to a direct salesperson as soon as the territory has reached a certain size.

Internet sales may also pose a dilemma because the direct sales may be perceived as a threat. Many companies will use their Web sites to provide information to customers but then put them in contact with a distributor near them for the actual sale.

Owens Corning faced conflict when it attempted to reduce its dependence on traditional sales channels and get closer to consumers by setting up home-improvement contracting kiosks in some Lowe's stores. Home remodeling contractors—a significant existing channel for the manufacturer—viewed the move as an unacceptable threat, and within a couple of years, Owens Corning discontinued the program. Now the company is testing another direct program by focusing on "handyman jobs" (such as basement remodeling or fixing a leaky faucet) rather than roofing and siding jobs that would compete with its traditional contractor customer base.[6] By focusing the new direct channels on a different end-use application, conflict was reduced.

Conflict between Different Channels

Sometimes conflict occurs when there are different channels to different customer groups (e.g., consumer vs. commercial channels), at different price points (e.g., specialty vs. general channels), or for different usage situations (e.g., convenience vs. full-support channels). Suppliers may provide different products or brands to the different channels (e.g., Black & Decker to retail channels and DeWalt to professional channels).

Levi Strauss & Company has attempted to revive its brand by selling different styles at different prices through a range of retailers. After traditionally selling its Levi's Red Tab at middle-tier outlets for $27-$35, it has added brands at both the high- and low-end channels. Levi Strauss Signature is sold through mass outlets like Wal-

Mart for about $23, and Levi's Vintage is being offered at high-end stores priced from $85 to $220.[7] The different brands and price points are being used to minimize conflicts across channels.

> **What mix of channels are best for my identified target markets?**
> ▶ Have I established a fair program for dealing with house accounts?
> ▶ Have I considered the impact of new channels on my relationship with existing channels?
> ▶ Can I use different brands, prices, and product strategies to reduce conflict between channels?

Building Hybrid Channels

Sometimes the best way to satisfy end-user needs is to create your own hybrid channel. For example, some companies that have traditionally sold to and through residential contractors are finding consumer's strong connections with retailers such as Home Depot are forcing a reevaluation of the channel design. Trane (a manufacturer of heating and air conditioning equipment) and Home Depot are experimenting with a program that positions Home Depot as a lead generation partner within Trane's channel. Home Depot has agreed to display Trane's residential equipment in select geographic areas as a lead generator for participating Trane dealer/contractors.[8] This type of hybrid channel attempts to capitalize on advantages of different channel types without causing undue conflict.

Creating hybrid channels is actually an elaboration of the examination of functionality that was introduced in Table 6-1, but the process can go beyond to include not only traditional channel partners but also the other facilitating intermediaries that offer services to channel members. For instance, banks play a key role in managing credit and collections for order processing, whether for the seller, buyer, and/or the outsourced services that these trading partners utilize to create value for customers and end users. Other examples include promotion and advertising agencies that aid in demand creation, logistics services providers that aid in fulfilling order and shipment delivery, customs brokers that aid buyers and sellers in satisfying border crossing requirements, and distributors that aid in creating demand, providing technical services, fulfilling demand, and handling credit and collections settlements.

Examples of outsourced functionality to nontraditional partners are discussed below.

1. **Banks** work to affect cash settlements between parties when firms are involved in supplier-managed, consigned inventories. The bank will work as an agent in capturing sales for a period of time and then make payments on behalf of the buyer at specified times in compliance with a three-party contract among the seller, buyer, and the bank(s). The role of banks is especially critical in international distribution when dealing with foreign parties and currencies.

2. **Logistics services providers** affect order and shipment fulfillment processes for making products available from sellers to buyers at agreed-upon points of usage or sale and to meet other performance requirements as agreed upon in statements of work or expectations.

3. **Grocery retail chains** often use supplier-provided rack-jobber services, or multiple suppliers may use outsourced services to stock racks for multiple lines in a product-line category. As an example, TLC, Inc. from Zeeland, Michigan, works with the dairy category of products to maximize the profitability of Meijer's retail outlets. TLC provides the coordination with the category manager, such as Dean Foods, along with other suppliers to the dairy section of the stores. Along with managed outsourced services, TLC also can provide software. Many logistics services providers, such as UPS, also offer financial services to the channel partners.

4. **IT providers** are now providing interfacing services between buyers and sellers in improving the information exchanges between sellers, buyers, and also logistics services providers. In today's environment, IT providers now offer consulting and software products along with outsourced services (including maintenance and upgrades) to actually manage IT departments and operational functionality among trading partners.

Note that the lines are blurring among distributors, banks and financial institutions, logistics services providers, and information technology providers in providing services between manufacturers and users of products. These parties are now performing on-demand operational services, software sales, Web-based services, and process improvement consulting, plus other functional and technical out-sourced services.

Information technology providers have recognized that their services must be accompanied by consulting services and outsourced operational services that go beyond software sales and maintenance agreements. Buyers want implemented, successful solutions.

So why should a firm outsource various functional and technical capabilities to outside organizations? Review the pros and cons of the outsourcing of various functional and technical capabilities in Table 6-2. On the positive side, companies may outsource noncore functions to allow them to concentrate on core competencies. On the negative side, outsourcing may result in loss of control and less direct end-customer contact.

A key consideration in outsourcing is that the buyer and/or seller are still held responsible for performance with the risks of outsourcing dependent upon the agency relationships with the outsourced organization. Integration skills and ultimate performance responsibility are still key considerations that cannot be outsourced.

As firms move to improve channel performance, third-party intermediaries who act as agents for the firm are often used to implement these channel pursuits. In the food industry, a concept of category management at the retailer level has as its basis the designation of an enterprise becoming the category manager for a section of the retail store. The category manager has a shared responsibility with the retailer in managing the profitability of, for instance, the dairy section of a supermarket. One company is picked as the category manager or leader who then must work with other suppliers in pursuing improved profitability for the dairy section. As the firm reviews the tasks and functionality to meet consumer needs in the dairy section, the selected firm and primary trading partners may not have the most economical process of keeping the shelves full.

An alternative is to enlist the aid of a third-party logistics services provider to work with the channel managers and associated suppliers in marshalling supplies to the front lines and the shelves.

Pros	Cons
• Aid in strategic planning, tactical deployment of services, and operations execution • Concentrate on core competencies • Leverage knowledge in industry • Deliver best and most current technology • Agile gain immediate, additional resources and assistance • Reduce labor and management costs • Less demand on capital • Share rewards and risks.	• Loss of control • Security issues • Increased variable costs • Less ability to direct human resources • Loss of design expertise • Less direct customer contact • More variability in customer service

Table 6-2. Strategic outsourcing and alliances: why outsource and form alliances?

This same approach is being used for industrial commodities, health care, and other industries.

One last point considering these outsourced relationships is contractual. How are these relationships constructed legally and commercially? These legal relationships can become entangling when considering that more than two parties are involved. Legal counsel needs to be involved in making sure that performance expectations are reflected in contractual agreements and no antitrust or discriminatory actions are taking place. Detailed statements of expectations (SOEs) or statements of work (SOWs) with assumed responsibilities and risks must be established and delineated among channel partners.

Reflection Point

Have I disaggregated my channel(s) into their component functions, services, and activities to look for improvements?

▶ Can I use different channels for different parts of the sales process in a way that minimizes conflict?

▶ Can I build a superior channel to my end customers by outsourcing some of these functions to nontraditional channel partners?

▶ Will this disaggregation provide superior benefits to the end customers and to the channel partners?

Key Points

▶ Determine what you want the *results* of your channel design to be before you begin to make the changes.

▶ Decide if you can attain your goals with your existing channel structure. If so, leverage your channel structure to maximum advantage.

▶ If new channels need to be added, establish trust before making changes, then create strategies to minimize channel conflict.

▶ Continually test new ways of sharing resources and capabilities throughout the channel so you are able to meet your end-customers' most extraordinary needs.

Notes

1. Donald V. Fites, "Making Your Dealers Your Partners," *Harvard Business Review,* March-April 1996, pp. 84-95.
2. Steven Burke, "Clear Policies Help Ease Channel Conflict," *CRN,* 8 April 2002, p. 20.
3. James A. Narus and James C. Anderson, "Rethinking Distribution," *Harvard Business Review*, July-August 1996, pp. 112-120.
4. Pat Curry, "Channel Changes," *Industry Week*, 2 April 2001, pp. 45-48.
5. "Forces of Change in the Distribution Channel," Lehman Health Care Distribution and Technology Hot Topics Conference Call, December 12, 2002, www.lehman.com.
6. Dale Buss, "Crossing the Channel," *Sales & Marketing Management*, October 2002, pp. 42-48.
7. Sally Beatty, "Mass Levi's, Class Levi's," *The Wall Street Journal*, 31 October 2002, pp. B1-B3.
8. Hall, John R., "Selling through the 'Big Box'," *Air Conditioning, Heating & Refrigeration News*, 28 October 2002, pp. 1, 26.

Chapter 7

INTERNATIONAL CHANNEL DESIGN

Domestic channel design issues were covered in the previous chapter, and many of the same principles also apply to international channels. However, there are some differences, and this chapter will focus on those differences.

Targeting World Markets

Just as domestic channel design should start with an examination of corporate goals, international channel design should begin with an objective market (i.e., country) and goal assessment prior to deciding on international distribution. There are several issues a firm must address when deciding to compete internationally. Part of the global strategy involves deciding which activities in the value chain (e.g., sourcing, production, distribution) should be handled in the United States and which in other nations. Then you must decide whether these activities will be handled by company-owned facilities or through alliances with other organizations.

The market assessment should determine which countries or regions provide the greatest potential for your products and services. The product strategy should specify whether the goods will be sold as standard global products; as standard core products with regional options, features, and changes; or as uniquely configured products in different regions.[1]

There are few truly global products. Consequently, because some degree of change is required, the manufacturer must decide whether the changes will be made domestically or through international channel partners.

International strategy requires good market data, but it is harder to obtain than domestic information. Some of the common sources of information, along with their Web sites, are listed in Table 7-1. A good starting point is www.export.gov, which is the U.S. government portal to exporting and trade services. It provides links to a number of other government agencies that are partners in its mission.

▶ The World Bank Group
  www.worldbank.org/
▶ U.S. Department of Commerce, International Trade Administration
  www.ita.doc.gov/td/tic/
▶ National Association of Manufacturers
  www.nam.org/
▶ Agency for International Development
  www.usaid.gov/about_usaid/
▶ U.S. Customs Service (now part of Department of Homeland Security)
  www.CBP.gov/
▶ Export Administration Regulations
  w3.access.gpo.gov/bis/index.html
▶ Various international trade statistics available from the U.S. government
  www.stat-usa.gov/miscfiles.nsf/TO?OpenView
▶ World Trade Centers Association
  iserve.wtca.org/
▶ Economist country briefings
  www.economist.com/countries/
▶ Department of Agriculture
  www.usda.gov/

Table 7-1. International information sources (continued on next page)

- ▶ Department of State
  www.state.gov/
- ▶ U.S. Government Export Portal
  www.export.gov/
- ▶ American Association of Exporters & Importers
  www.aaei.org/events/event.asp?event_id=183
- ▶ Directory of American Firms Operating in Foreign Countries
  www.uniworldbp.com/af_main.shtml
- ▶ *International Trade Statistics Yearbook*
  Published by the United Nations and available through major university libraries
- ▶ National Trade Data Bank (U.S. Dept. of Commerce)
  govpubs.lib.umn.edu/stat/tool_ntdb.phtml
- ▶ United Nations
  www.un.org/
- ▶ International Monetary Fund
  www.imf.org/

Table 7-1. International information sources (continued)

Reflection Point

Do I have a global business strategy that is the basis for my channel strategy?
- ▶ Am I prepared to deal with many of the channel issues, government regulations, cultural aspects, and business opportunities associated with doing business with other nations?
- ▶ Does my organization understand the major risks and responsibilities of going international?
- ▶ Have I examined the additional costs of doing business internationally?
- ▶ Can I grow the business profitably while incurring the added responsibilities and costs of going international?

Evaluating Different International Channel Structures

Once the country priorities are determined as part of the overall strategy, manufacturers will need to make decisions on channel design as was discussed in the previous two chapters. However, there are subtly different types of intermediaries for international distribution that should be defined. Most firms initially enter other countries through either indirect or direct exporting.

Indirect exporting refers to selling through a domestically based intermediary (e.g., agent or distributor). The major benefits of this approach lie in the ease of administration. Even companies with little or no experience in exporting can rely on the expertise of the channel partner without developing substantial multinational cultural skills.

With direct exporting, the manufacturer deals directly with foreign intermediaries in the distribution of its products. While this approach requires a greater degree of cultural expertise, it also provides the company with more market knowledge and potentially greater control. A listing of types of direct and indirect intermediaries is provided in Table 7-2.

Foreign (Direct)	Domestic (Indirect)
Agents	
Brokers Manufacturers' Reps Management Agents	Brokers Manufacturers' Export Agents Export Management Companies
Distributors	
Distributors Dealers Import Jobbers Wholesalers and Retailers	Domestic Wholesalers Export Merchants Complementary Marketers Export Jobbers
Other Partners	
Licensees Franchisees Contract Manufacturers	

Table 7-2. International channel intermediaries

In addition to determining whether the best location for the intermediary is domestic or foreign, it is useful to examine the differences between agent, distributor, and other intermediaries. Agents, brokers, manufacturer's reps and export management companies (EMCs) generally *do not* take title to the products they represent. Distributors, dealers, jobbers, wholesalers, and merchants generally *do* take title. The *other partners* listed either have varied contractual relations with the manufacturer or provide specific differential functions.[2]

When licensing is used as an entry strategy, the manufacturer assigns the right to a patent or trademark to a foreign company. The advantage of this approach is that some governments may prefer it. The disadvantage is the manufacturer's dependence on the licensee.

Franchising is a form of licensing agreement whereby the manufacturer grants to the foreign company the rights to do business in a prescribed manner. This has similar advantages and disadvantages to licensing, but because the franchise agreement is more comprehensive than a licensing agreement, the manufacturer has somewhat more control.

Under contract manufacturing, a company arranges to have its products manufactured by a foreign firm under a contractual basis. The manufacturing may involve assembly or fully integrated production, depending on the needs of the firm.

Reflection Point

Have I assessed the roles of alternative international channel members—both direct and indirect—in business development?

▶ Have I evaluated the advantages and disadvantages of the various types of international channel types?

▶ Have I determined the level of control necessary to implement my distribution strategy in other countries?

Selecting the Right Channel Partners

Whether dealing with direct or indirect channel partners, it is important to find top representatives. Tactics and the rules of the game in managing international channel operations must be established for adaptation of the organization and products to foreign cultures and politics. Employees working in functional areas of research and development, finance, marketing, pricing, legal, manufacturing, purchasing, transportation, and logistics must be trained in international business; and cross-functional teams must be established to implement international business development strategies and processes for execution.

Several sources exist for locating international trading partners. Global associations exist by country, and with the Internet, it is a relatively easy task to tap private and government databases for prospective business partners. In addition to private databases and services, some of which are associated with industry trade associations, business managers can explore state and national government databases. Databases plus government country and commodity specialists and U.S. senatorial offices can aid the international seller in sourcing and promoting international business development.

A couple of services of the U.S. Department of Commerce are especially helpful. The Agent Distributor Service finds foreign firms that are interested and qualified to represent given manufacturers. Trade missions involve groups of U.S. executives, led by federal and state commerce departments, that travel to meet with potential foreign channel partners.

Finally, the Internet can be instrumental in locating potential foreign trade partners. Through private and public posting services, firms can advertise if they are looking for prospective international trading partners. You post your ad, and then you can source, qualify, and select those partners that best meet your needs while meeting their needs.

As will be discussed in Chapter 8, which is about how to select domestic business partners, there are some common criteria that deal with both domestic and international partner selection. In his *Harvard Business Review* article, David Arnold states that the selection of international business partners is especially critical because of distances and cultures of the buying parties.[3] He elaborates on these seven key points in selecting and working with international distributors and trading partners.

1. "Select distributors. Don't let them select you." Key information regarding this point is to be market-led, selecting distributors and agents who support the seller's market-driven strategy. Be systematic and conduct a thorough assessment of potential partners utilizing objective selection criteria as illustrated in Table 7-3. These selection criteria will aid manufacturers in developing and using a formal process for trading partner selection, assessment of performance, and recognition of absolute

and improved performance. As the saying goes, how we are measured and recognized drives how we perform.

2. "Look for distributors capable of developing markets, rather than those with a few obvious customer contacts." In effect, select partners who are willing to invest and develop customer relationships that are most appropriate for the manufacturer in marketing its own products and growing markets.

3. "Treat the local distributors as long-term partners, not temporary market-entry vehicles." Create an atmosphere and agreements with strong incentives for appropriate goals, such as customer acquisition and retention, new product sales, collaborative inventory management and replenishment.

4. "Support market entry by committing money, managers, and proven marketing ideas." Invest in product modifications to meet the needs of local markets and have market and product managers meet with the distributors to share new ideas and past success strategies.

5. "From the start, maintain control over marketing strategy." Firms should convene and lead planning and budgeting sessions, even sending a few employees to work full-time at the local distributor's offices to oversee distributor performance in meeting customer needs.

6. "Make sure distributors provide you with detailed market and financial performance data." Develop relationships and contracts that share detailed market data and financial performance. Not having this information can lead to serious problems in providing and servicing products to meet customer needs by business and geographic segments or customer categories.

7. "Build links among national distributors at the earliest opportunity." Just as in the United States, distributors meet and build relationships to share experiences. Rather than letting the distributors build their own relationships helter-skelter, take overt actions to facilitate their interactions and draw upon the experiences of all distributors to maximize returns of all parties.

Once corporations understand that they can control their international operations through better relationship structures rather than simply through ownership, they might also find longer-term roles for local distributors with a regionalized approach to global strategy.

A key point in selecting international trading partners—as well as any distributor or trading partner—is to develop sound, objective selection criteria, as listed in Table 7-3. Column 1 illustrates a list of selection criteria with column 2 giving examples of how scales and weighting factors for each criteria need to be determined.

A manual should be developed to go along with these criteria and scales—defining what you mean by the criteria and the weight given to that factor in selecting an OUSA partner.

For example, if a U.S. firm is selecting one or more distributors or other intermediaries to serve the European Union (EU), it must assess whether the prospect serves the target country, such as Germany, as well as other bordering countries. If so, the firm could get a 5 on the scale if it has extensive national coverage.

If the firm has coverage that is not completely consistent with the market coverage desired by the manufacturer, the rating would be lower. If the prospect serves all of the EU, then the firm would get a 5 if that is of high priority to the firm.

For each of the possible selection criteria in Column 1, the firm would assign relative weights, with heavier weights going to those that are most important to the firm. The weights should total to 100 percent. The individual factor ratings would be multiplied by the respective weights, then added to arrive at a weighted score.

The use of these objective selection criteria is important in:

- ▶ building consensus of the firm's business development team
- ▶ providing feedback to prospective partners as to why they were or were not selected
- ▶ developing and improving channel partner performance for both the manufacturer and the distributors and other trading partners
- ▶ recognizing performance through objective measures, perhaps contained in statements of work or expectations

When negotiating with potential channel partners, it is important to remember two iron rules of international business. First, the seller is expected to adapt to the buyer (and because you are selling to the distributor, you will need to do the adapting).

Key Areas of Evaluation	Criteria and Weights		
✓ International coverage as to countries, race, cultures ✓ National coverage in targeted markets ✓ Knowledge of the marketplace ✓ Not afraid to invest in customers ✓ Complementary product lines ✓ Stable political climate ✓ Not afraid to make changes to operations ✓ Use information and communications technology ✓ Financially strong ✓ Professional stable management ✓ Low employee turnover ✓ Quality is part of business philosophy and culture	• Market Coverage • Knowledge • Investment • Product Lines • Political Climate • Change Potential • Information Use • Financial Strength • Management • Turnover • Quality	_____% _____% _____% _____% _____% _____% _____% _____% _____% _____% _____%	0 1 2 3 4 5 0 1 2 3 4 5 0 1 2 3 4 5 0 1 2 3 4 5 0 1 2 3 4 5 0 1 2 3 4 5 0 1 2 3 4 5 0 1 2 3 4 5 0 1 2 3 4 5 0 1 2 3 4 5 0 1 2 3 4 5
	Total Weighted Score (sum)	_____	

Table 7-3. Example criteria for selecting international channel partners

Second, the visitor is expected to observe local customs. These rules compel an understanding of the different types of cultures that exist in different parts of the world. Richard Gesteland, in his book, *Cross-Cultural Business Behavior*, provides a thorough discussion of four types of cultural continua, as shown in Figure 7-1.[4] The first addresses the business perspective ranging from deal-focused to relationship-focused. Distributors from relationship-focused cultures want to build a trusting relationship with a manufacturer prior to commencing business, and can perceive a deal-focused presentation as aggressive and pushy.

The second continuum is from formal to informal. *Informal* business managers typically come from relatively egalitarian cultures (like the United States) and sometimes make the mistake of not respecting the formality present in other cultures.

The third continuum is from rigid-time to fluid-time. Cultures that are driven by "the clock" may inappropriately perceive other cultures as lazy, resulting in tense and uncomfortable meetings. The final type of continuum is from expressive to reserved. Reserved cultures demonstrate conservative communication both verbally and nonverbally, and can therefore "clash" with people from expressive cultures.

It is important that manufacturers who are establishing relationships with international channel partners understand and appreciate the cultural differences so that trust can be established and negotiations can run smoothly.

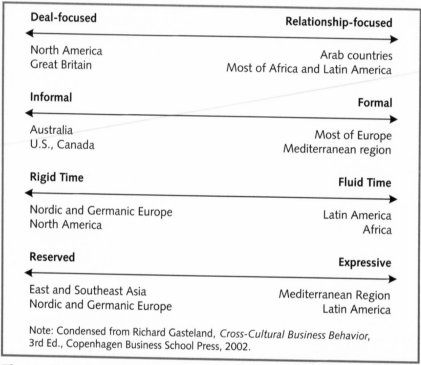

Note: Condensed from Richard Gasteland, *Cross-Cultural Business Behavior*, 3rd Ed., Copenhagen Business School Press, 2002.

Figure 7-1. Example of cultural divides in international negotiations

Have I invested sufficient time and energy in selecting the right representatives for my global channel strategies?

▶ Have I used all of the government and private sources available to improve the selection process?

▶ Are my people properly trained to handle international business?

▶ How well have I identified partners who are capable of developing the market for my products and attaining my objectives?

▶ Do I acquire a knowledge of the relevant business customs and ethics before negotiating a contract in a given world region?

Managing the Channel

At least three primary aspects of international channel management are different from domestic channel management. First is the existence of cross-cultural differences between the companies, as mentioned in the previous section. Second is the increased complexity resulting from different laws and regulations and the greater geographic distance. And finally, there is the increased concern over gray markets or parallel importation. Each of these must be considered in managing the channel.

Cross-cultural differences play a role not only in the initial "honeymoon" stage, but also throughout the management process. U.S. managers should not only learn about the customs in the areas where they are distributing, but if possible, should bring select channel partners to the United States to observe their domestic operations. Properly planned quarterly meetings—if not in person then through video and telephone conferencing—can provide the basis for performance evaluation and opportunities for improvement.

Distance is a nemesis to managing many international operations. At the outset, establish key result areas of performance. At the root of business intelligence is good data that is timely and has integrity. Be aware that delays occur in getting data. Determine data requirements necessary to measure outcomes and performance at the transactional level as well as the strategic level. Good transactional data that is obtained on a timely basis provides the foundation for sound operational control. This database can then feed tactical planning and strategic planning to measure the performance of international trading parties. Prioritizing areas of improvement opportunities leads to action planning that addresses critical items followed by actions to address "B" and "C" items of priority.

Finally, the special problem of gray markets should be monitored. Gray markets, or parallel importation, refer to the diversion of products produced or distributed abroad back to the United States—bypassing designated channels. The products are not counterfeit goods or copies, but they still take business away from products sold through domestic channels. A study reported in the *International Marketing Review* highlighted the concerns over the issue.

Marketers are cognizant that parallel imports can have a profound impact on the performance of a multinational company. Gray markets have been found to erode trademark image, destroy customer goodwill, trouble channel member relations, and disrupt global planning efforts ... When companies are forced to compete against their own trademarked items, profits decrease, prohibiting domestic distributors from continued promotion of the product. Goodwill established by the trademark owner is lost as consumers purchasing the parallel imports do not receive the same "extended product" (i.e. product usage information, service, warranty, and safety protection) ... Gray markets are significant as they now exceed $10 billion per year in North America and affect almost every major trademarked product. [Experts] counsel that the loss of control associated with gray markets can only be regained through an aggressive deterrent strategy. [5]

Although not everyone agrees that gray markets are a problem, they can impact a firm's strategies and should be considered when managing global operations.

Reflection Point

Am I fully cognizant of the unique challenges of managing global distribution channels?

▶ How knowledgeable am I of the cultural business behaviors of my channel partners, and how well do I adapt?

▶ Do I keep in regular contact with the channel via phone, e-mail or in-person visits?

▶ Have I evaluated the potential for gray markets for my products?

Key Points

▶ Establish your global growth strategy prior to developing international channels.

▶ Develop a desired distributor profile and then use it to identify appropriate distributors in the targeted world regions.

▶ Treat the local distributors as channel partners and provide relevant support.

▶ Monitor performance through two-way dialog with your channel.

► Consider all channels and the many organizations available to you in going international.

► Take advantage of the many government assistance programs at the federal and state levels.

► Be extremely careful and objective in selecting your associated trading partners.

► Use the many tools available to monitor how well your international strategies and demand management operations are being executed.

Notes

1. See Linda Gorchels, *The Product Manager's Field Guide* (McGraw-Hill, 2003, pp. 101-104) for a brief discussion of global product management issues.

2. Several sources provide more detailed information on international intermediaries. Chapter 11 of Louis W. Stern, Adel I. El-Ansary, and Anne T. Coughlan, *Marketing Channels, 5th ed.* (Prentice Hall, 1996) provides several tables comparing the different duties of the intermediaries. Chapter 12 of Michael R. Czinkota and Ilkka A. Ronkainen, *International Marketing, 4th ed.* (Dryden, 1995) provides some tips on screening intermediaries.

3. David Arnold, "Seven Rules of International Business, *Harvard Business Review,* November–December 2000, pp. 131-137.

4. Richard R. Gesteland, *Cross-Cultural Business Behavior, 3rd ed.* (Copenhagen Business School Press, 2002). The book provides a clear explanations and case examples of working with business people throughout the world.

5. Irvine Clarke III and Margaret Owens, "Trademark Rights in Gray Markets," *International Marketing Review*, Vol. 17, No. 3, 2000, p. 272.

Chapter 8

SELECTING SUITABLE CHANNEL PARTNERS

How much is the *right* channel partner worth to you? Managers may feel rushed into filling vacancies and therefore gloss over selection criteria. The outcome can be an improper match with distributors, dealers, or reps, yielding second-rate results.

Before you can select the right channel members, you will need to develop a profile of what is the ideal for your specific situation. In Chapter 5, you evaluated what your target customers want from a channel—the specific services and support that define the ideal. Now think in terms of "buying" these distribution services from resellers (rather than simply selling through them). What services would you want to "buy"? Then look for the type of channel that would "fit." Chances are you will need a mix of different types of channels to provide the requisite services.

After designing the channel mix and deciding on the right *type* of distributors or reps, the next stage is to search, assess, recruit, and sign the best channel partners. Note that the terms distributor, dealer, rep, and so forth will be used somewhat interchangeably in this chapter because many of the concepts apply generically. (In other words, *distributor* may be used to refer to any type of channel member.) Where there are specific differences between types of channel intermediaries, the differences will be specified. This chapter focuses on Stage IV of the process as shown in Figure 8-1.

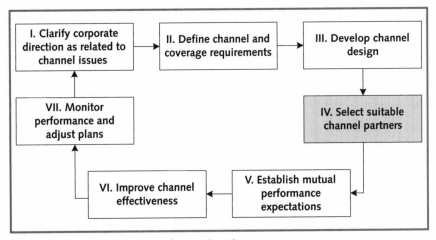

Figure 8-1. Stage IV in channel redesign

Search Methodology

You should consider several sources when looking for channel members. For most business products, an important source would be referrals from key customers and specifiers. Find out what distributors and reps they currently deal with and/or would like to deal with in the future.

Check directories of distributors and dealers for candidates in the geographic areas of interest. Many directories are provided through associations in which distributors are members. For example, the National Association of Wholesale Distributors (www.naw.org) has more than 100 national line-of-trade associations. These member associations represent virtually all products that move to market via wholesaler-distributors. The list also contains approximately 50 regional, state, and local wholesale distribution associations. Many companies will become members or associate members of the most appropriate associations to gain access to relevant channel information and member lists (i.e., potential candidates).

If you are looking for independent reps or manufacturers agents, a possible source is the Manufacturers' Agents National Association (www.manaonline.org). The association provides an online directory of reps both domestically and in Europe. Another association providing a directory is the Manufacturers' Representatives Educational Research Foundation (www.mrerf.org). This group provides training and certification for reps. Also, many industries have separate associations of rep members such as the Association of Independent Manufacturers'/Representatives, Inc. (www.aimr.net) which is a trade association of independent sales representatives in the plumbing, heating, cooling, and piping industry. Talk to a few reps to pinpoint the best association, then contact the association for a rep directory.

The manufacturers of compatible products can also be a source of channel information. By talking to noncompeting companies targeting similar customers, you can obtain names of distributors or reps who might be appropriate for your particular products and services. These channel members might be interested in carrying your products, or they might be able to refer you to other appropriate companies.

What to Look For

As you gather the names of possible channel partners, you must begin assessing their fit for your needs. It's important to remember that the channel members are independent businesses with their own goals, plans, key customers, existing product lines, and capabilities. Although some may be willing to make changes for an important supplier (principal), it is usually better to look for as much compatibility as possible between their existing business profile and your ideal partner profile. In other words, unless you are a highly strategic supplier to the channel members, they will unlikely be willing to change their business processes to provide what you want.

Begin by developing an ideal candidate template as shown in Figure 8-2. The second column should contain a description of the ideal distributor along each of the factors listed. A discussion of some of the considerations follows.

Market Served. The accounts and/or types of customers currently served should match your desired end users. This is particularly important for independent reps where part of what you are "buying" is the market contacts. Distinguish between generic customer lists and active accounts.

Also, determine the depth of market knowledge the candidate has—both in terms of current customers and pending account changes. Does the candidate specialize in vertical or horizontal mar-

	Description of Ideal	Candidate Evaluation
Market Served		
Product Line Fit		
Territorial Coverage		
Sales Capabilities		
Business and Managerial Stability		
Marketing Capabilities		
Operational Capabilities		
Local Service		
Ease of Doing Business		
Reputation		
Other		

Describe your "ideal" distributor here.

Compare your candidate to the "ideal" here.

Figure 8-2. Ideal candidate template

kets, or sell to all customers within the geography? Does this type of coverage fit your strategic plan?

Product Line Fit. The types of products carried should enhance your offering to the end user. Look for complementary offerings (especially for reps). Who are their existing suppliers? Channel members who carry complementary products are more likely to be reaching the customers you want to reach.

On the other hand, many distributors will carry competing products. Determine whether the products are from primary competitors, and if so, whether it still makes sense to pursue the candidate.

Territorial Coverage. Compare the distributor's trading area with the coverage gap in your channel design. Does it close the gap? Is there overlap with other territories? This evaluation should also consider the presence of or potential for branch locations and the impact that has on territorial coverage. Stocking branch locations can increase the effective size of the territory, but the process might also cause conflict with other distributors.

Sales Capabilities. Define whether you desire channel members with an emphasis on business development or account maintenance. When considering distributors, you would want to examine the sales force structure and determine whether they have the technical capability to sell your product. What is the number of inside and outside sales representatives? This figure may give you some indication of the emphasis on order-taking versus proactive selling. What type of training and incentives do the sales reps have? Are these consistent with industry expectations?

When examining reps, look at the technical capabilities and knowledge of the salespeople in the agency. Is an engineering background required? What type of prior sales skills are necessary? If prospecting is required, have the salespeople demonstrated that skill? Is technical certification important to sales success? How do the salespeople deal with competition? Ride along on a couple of customer calls to assess sales performance.

Business and Managerial Stability. Look at the performance history of the company. Specifically examine financial performance, including timely bill payment and sales of complementary products. Have there been significant fluctuations in sales and profit? If the company is privately owned, is there a succession plan in place? Do the candidate's growth prospects fit your strategic plan? How high is the employee turnover rate and why? Are there training programs in place for employees?

Marketing Capabilities. How important is it that the channel promote and create demand for your product? Does the candidate have these skills? Is the company willing to push new products?

Operational Capabilities. Depending on the needs of your product, you may require specific warehousing capacity, logistics facilities, repair and service competence, e-commerce experience, customer training programs, or other services. Assess whether the candidate's operational capabilities are sufficient for your product goals in the territory. Tour the facilities to get a feel for the candidate's operational strengths and weaknesses.

Local Services. Will your product require (or will your end users demand) services such as installation, technical support, credit, immediate parts availability, warranty execution, loaner products, turnkey operations, product assembly, or other local services? How strong is the candidate in these services? What is the order fulfillment rate?

Ease of Doing Business. Although "chemistry" is generally not the most critical factor in the selection process, it may influence the ease of doing business with the candidate. How well do you get along with the owners, management team, and employees of the candidate firm? Is the firm willing to sign a performance contract with you? Does the candidate have a true desire to handle your product line? Is there mutual trust?

Reputation. Determine the candidate's reputation among customers, other manufacturers, and peers.

Reflection Point

How well do I prepare to search for new distributors?

▶ Do I use several sources to find new leads or fall back on the way I've always done it?

▶ Do I develop a template to use when conducting the search?

▶ Does the template include the types of services I would like to buy to better meet end-customer needs?

Assessing Your Channel Candidate

No distributor (or rep) can meet all of the requirements listed earlier. Priorities must be set. Therefore, a little preplanning can go a long way. It may be useful to establish a template that details the specifics of the ideal candidate as just described and use it to evaluate each candidate. The evaluation of each candidate would be provided in the final column of Figure 8-2.

The template and your determination of the distributors' fit are qualitative or subjective evaluations. However, that does not imply unstructured. The very act of developing the profile will help provide a focus for your further discussions with the candidates. And the template may help you decide whether you need a generalist or a specialist, a traditional channel, or a hybrid channel.

Distributors can exist along a continuum from generalist to specialist. (See Figure 8-3.) Generalist (or broad-line) distributors carry a large assortment of products from multiple suppliers. Similar to Wal-Mart in the consumer arena, generalist distributors focus on rapid turnover of fast-moving parts. They typically have a catalog of offerings and limited sales support.

Specialist Distributors	Generalist Distributors
←————————————————————————————————→	
Product Specialists	Product Generalists
Full Parts Inventory	Fast-moving Inventory
Pro-active Selling	Reactive Selling
Dedicated Resources	Heavy Inventory Resources
Fewer, Larger Customer Orders	Many Customer Orders

Figure 8-3. Distributor continuum

Specialists, on the other hand, focus on a more defined market offering, which frequently requires extensive sales effort and technical knowledge. Products in the early stages of a market life cycle benefit from the additional support allotted by specialist channels, whereas products later in the life cycle benefit from the mass reach and exposure afforded by generalists.

Sometimes product and/or market requirements do not fit neatly into any particular channel type. When that's the case, it may be necessary to create a hybrid channel and assess a channel candidate on its ability to contribute to a particular activity in the hybrid channel. Start by splitting the activities of the channel into presale, sales transaction, and postsale activities.

Candidates who will be involved in presales activities are primarily lead generation partners. As mentioned in Chapter 5, Home Depot can serve as a lead generation partner for various contractors. The sales transaction may be handled by independent reps, a firm's direct sales force, or distributor salespeople. Postsales activities include delivery, installation, repair, warranty work, etc. Sometimes service partners are added to a channel to focus exclusively on these postsale activities.

Recruit and Sign the Best Candidates

After reducing the list of distributors to those you would most likely want to work with (i.e., those closest to the ideal on your template), you need to establish a good dialogue with those candidates. It is useful at this point to think like a distributor (see Chapter 9). What you see as a product worth $2,000 is just a box worth $60 in margin for the distributor. You are not selling them the product per se but rather you are selling them the chance to earn the margin and the belief that your company will provide the product and support necessary for them to gain that margin.

Identify the key people in the distributorship and think about the information you want to share with them as well as what questions you think they will ask you. In general, you will want to discuss your current go-to-market strategies, along with your business goals as they relate to the channel. Who are your end-user segments, and what is your competitive advantage with them? What are your marketing plans in terms of new product launches and promotional communications? What expectations do you have of your channel in terms of quotas, and what compensation and supporting services do you provide?

The distributor will ask you questions as well. Typical questions will include the following:

▶ What types of services will be expected in terms of inventory, installation and repair, warranty work, missionary sales, etc.?
▶ Will I have unrestricted access to new products?
▶ How are national accounts handled, and what impact will that have on my compensation?
▶ How many distributors potentially serve my customers, and are there plans to add new distributors?
▶ What type of training will be available for me?
▶ Who do I call when there is a problem?
▶ What rights do I have to use the supplier's brand logo?

It is important to have a clear, objective perspective on the importance of your product to the channel. (See Figure 8-4.) If your product is strategically significant to the distributor, you will have much more power and influence than if your product is minor. Major products have high importance to distributors, to the point that their

	Major Products	Secondary Products	Minor Products
Importance to Distributor's Business	High	Moderate	Low
Distributor Willingness to Adapt	High	Moderate	Low
Manufacturer's Marketing Approach	Push	Push/Pull	Pull

Figure 8-4. Product importance categories

business is built around those products. Frank Lynn refers to these as *primary* products, accounting for 10 percent or more of total sales.[1]

Ken Rolnicki separates the major products into those of high importance (accounting for 10 percent of sales) and high strategic importance (accounting for 40 percent of sales).[2] Regardless of the exact percentages, your products are *major* if distributors will proactively sell them and even modify components of their business for you.

Secondary products account for approximately 5 percent of sales. Distributors will sell these products and use your support if it can be easily incorporated into their business. However, they are unlikely to make significant changes for the manufacturer. *Minor* products account for less than 1 percent of sales. Distributors will fill orders but not be willing to modify their business or actively sell for you.

The importance of your product has significance with regard to what will be important to the distributor in terms of negotiation. If your product will be a major addition to a distributor's line, the candidate will be concerned about channel conflict, future growth potential, training, logo usage, and similar issues of doing business. For secondary and minor products, the distributor will be more interested in how easy you are to do business with, what pull-through campaigns you have to generate orders, and the fit within their existing business.

Find out what is important to the distributor—what the company really wants or needs. As a starting point, you can be sure that the distributor will expect quality products, adequate compensation, and support from the manufacturer. Be prepared to provide proof that you have all three. Show statistical proof of your product line's quality standards and possibly verification from customers or other channels. Offer discounts and margins that are acceptable in the industry.

And don't forget that compensation is more than just the discount. It includes price elements such as discounts, rebates, and allowances but also cost elements such as freight terms, credit terms, and sales support. Highlight the most relevant support (e.g., cooperative advertising, fee-for-service programs, coaching, etc.) for the type of product (major, secondary, or minor).

Beyond these basics, prepare a list of enticements to use as necessary during the negotiation process. Don't present them all at once but offer them on an as-needed basis. Some possible enticements are discussed below.

Full-product Line Commitment. Distributors may want the flexibility of carrying any future products in your line and may value the promise that there will be no restrictions.

Rapid Delivery. Although rapid delivery can sometimes encourage last-minute orders, meeting emergency demands promptly is respected.

Drop-shipment Capability. If distributors are expected to satisfy local orders from inventory, drop-shipping may seem an inappropriate bargaining chip. However, for many bulky products, unique customer requests, or the need to expedite shipments from multiple locations, drop-shipping can be beneficial.

Price Protection. Offer to protect prices against fluctuations in inventory valuation. Distributors will want to keep inventory to a minimum for products that are declining in price or fluctuating widely. This can be a problem for manufacturers who need immediate product availability at the local level and for whom stock-outs cause lost orders. Providing price protection so that distributors will not lose value in the inventory they are carrying gives them more incentive to increase stock levels.

For example, if a distributor purchased product for inventory for $100,000 and the value of that inventory declined to $95,000 due to price concessions at the end-user level, the manufacturer could provide a $5,000 credit for future purchases.

First-class Warranty Program. Warranty programs that are superior to those offered by the competition are generally easier for distributors to sell to end customers. This may entice distributors to carry your product.

Superior Cooperative Advertising or Promotional Allowances.
Cooperative (co-op) advertising programs share the cost of local advertising of the manufacturer's product between the manufacturer and the distributor. Promotional allowances are generally provided as a rebate for money spent on local promotions. In either case, the amount of money available from the manufacturer varies by industry but is generally in the range of 1 to 5 percent of total purchases from that manufacturer.

Stock Rotation Programs. The handling of returns can be an issue between distributor and manufacturer. Product defects should be brought to the attention of the manufacturer, but what about slow-moving goods? Manufacturers will often accept back a certain amount of nonsaleable products when they are accompanied by a purchase order for new products of an equivalent or greater value.

Ride-along Sales Support. For certain key customers or major products, distributors may benefit from having a knowledgeable salesperson or product manager from the manufacturer join in a sales call.

Above-average Payment or Credit Terms. Superior terms may be given as a short-term enticement to sign the distributor.

Lead Generation and/or Qualification. If you have an ongoing telesales, advertising, or trade show program generating strong leads, you can offer an estimated number of territorial leads to the distributor.

Regional Warehousing. For some products, it makes sense for a manufacturer to have regional warehouses to service distributors. This can reduce the amount of inventory the distributor must carry and/or the lead time for orders without risking out-of-stock situations for the end user. This is a supply chain question.

Product Training. Although distributors want to know their products well enough to sell them successfully, they can accommodate training for only a few products—generally the major products. If your product will be major for the distributor, describe the relevant types of educational opportunities you will provide. If the product is secondary or minor, demonstrate how you will simplify or streamline the process of learning about the product.

Special Demonstration Equipment Policies. If demonstration is a critical part of the sales process for your product, think creatively about ways to facilitate the willingness of distributors to attain and utilize demonstration equipment.

As mentioned in Chapter 3, establishing a written distributor agreement or contract is wise. The contract specifies the mutual expectations of both parties and the business policies that will not change. In addition, there will be attachments or addenda that contain the territorial and market provisions, product provisions, and sales/performance expectations.

Reflection Point

How well do I prepare for candidate interviews?
▶ Do I consistently evaluate candidates according to the template I developed earlier?
▶ Have I identified the key people in the various distributorships?
▶ Am I prepared to discuss mutual performance expectations?
▶ Am I prepared with a list of negotiable items to use on an as-needed basis?

Key Points

▶ Selecting the right channel partners up front will improve the chances of long-term success.
▶ Think in terms of *buying* distribution, sales, and support services when developing a template of your preferred distributor.
▶ Clarify the type of distributor most apt to fit your template.
▶ Understand how important your product is likely to be to the distributor when preparing your approach.
▶ Be primed to discuss mutual performance expectations when interviewing channel candidates.
▶ Know in advance what is and is not negotiable.

Notes

1. Adapted from information from Frank Lynn & Associates, refer to www.franklynn.com.
2. Kenneth Rolnicki, *Managing Channels of Distribution* (Chicago: Amacom, 1998), p. 15.

Part Three
Managing the Ongoing Relationship

UNDERSTANDING THE DISTRIBUTOR'S WORLD:
Implications for Suppliers

The first step in building a good relationship with distributors is to understand their world, their current business pressures, their view of manufacturers, and the primary differences between a manufacturing business and a distribution business. A clear and full understanding of a distributor's financial imperatives, capabilities and rapidly changing business environment can assist manufacturers in developing more realistic expectations for distributor performance and more effective sales support programs.

Distributor Definitions

The word *distributor* means vastly different things to different people, as was mentioned in the previous chapter. There are two fundamentally different types of distributors. At one end of the distributor spectrum are *generalists* who provide a large number and variety of products to a defined geographic region. At the other end of the spectrum are the *specialists* who provide technical and application information about the few select products they carry.

Generalist distributors, such as W. W. Grainger, Inc., in Chicago, are known as wholesalers, general-line distributors, industrial distributors, or warehouse distributors. Their strength is product availability, customer relationships, and competitive pricing. The wide variety of products they offer prohibits full and in-depth product knowledge for each line offering.

Specialists are usually referred to by the type of business they are in, such as food-service equipment distributors or truck accessory distributors. They are traditionally strong in product and application knowledge and customer support services. However, they carry a narrow range of products and limited inventory.

There are several other definitions of distributor. Some insurance companies use the term to refer to their agents, producers, or aggregators. Other companies use the terms dealer and distributor interchangeably. Still other companies have premier versus affiliate distributors or different roles for those involved in one-step versus two-step distribution. All of these businesses are called *distributors* yet represent very different abilities to execute a manufacturer's marketing and sales program.

A distributor or distributorship should be defined functionally, that is, by the services it provides to customers and manufacturers. The word distributor, without further definition, can lead to misunderstanding and false expectations.

Reflection Point	**Where are my distributors on the continuum from specialist to generalist?** ▶ Do different distributors occupy different places on the continuum? ▶ Where is the ideal location on the continuum for my distributors? ▶ Does continuum location change for the different target markets I wish to serve?

Manufacturer's Influence

Manufacturers attempt to exert influence over their distributors to accomplish their sales and marketing goals. The degree of influence any manufacturer can exert on a distributor is directly proportional to the percentage of revenue and profit the manufacturer's product line generates for the distributor. (See Figure 8-4 in Chapter 8.)

A product generating a small percentage of business—about 1 percent—is considered a minor product line and is carried only to fill out customer orders. No manufacturer influence is possible. A secondary product line creates from 2 to 10 percent of total sales. Secondary lines are important to the distributor salespeople and the customers who routinely purchase those products. A major line, any line that represents more than 10 percent of total revenue or profit to the distributor, is an important line to the success of the distributorship and its ability to service key customers.

The manufacturer of a major product line can exert influence over the distributor's stocking levels, sales and promotion efforts, and operating methods. Minor and secondary line suppliers have much less success in exerting any influence over a distributor's behavior. In summary, your distributor relationship can vary from simple product availability with no leverage to a very high level of promotion, sales, stocking, and service support resulting from the manufacturer's leverage and involvement.

Reflection Point	**How can I exert more influence than my percentage of the distributor's business would normally allow?** ▶ What methods have worked the best? ▶ What methods did not work?

Forces of Change

The distributor's world has changed more in the past five years than it has changed in the previous 50 years. The key factors driving change are technological, social, and economic. The most obvious change has been technology. The speed and amount of information that can be exchanged via the Internet and e-mail are reducing the importance of geographic boundaries.

The increased speed and availability of transportation are further reducing the geographic boundaries, which previously defined a distributor's territory. Channel conflict for distributors today isn't the geographic boundary wars of 20 years ago. Today, the conflict can come from any location because of Internet product availability, international sourcing and pricing, and rapid drop-shipping from multiple locations.

Social trends, such as globalization of markets and social fluidity, cause markets to grow, shrink, shift, and subdivide at accelerating rates. Distributors have to learn to adapt to new markets and new customers more quickly than before. Change is difficult for distributors who have taken many years to establish positions of market dominance by selling and servicing customers with consistent product availability, credit, service support, and relationship-building events in a local geographic area.

Specialty distributors tend to be smaller and rely on product, application, and market expertise. Consequently, specialty distributors can change market direction more quickly than generalists can. However, a small market change can wipe out a specialty distributor in one selling season, while a generalist has more resources, time, and money for the required adaptations to take place. Both types of distributorships are challenged by change—but in very different ways. Manufacturers need to understand and assist distributors in adapting to rapid market change and their new battlefield for economic survival.

The third factor disrupting distribution is the economic turbulence we have experienced in the past five years. Historic retail business success stories such as Kmart, Montgomery Ward, and J.C. Penney, have fallen on economic hard times. Other businesses—from Wal-Mart and Home Depot to Marshall Field's and Macy's—have adapted well to the new economic realities. Distributors are feeling a similar turbulence from the economy and competitors.

Distributors are being forced to change their basic business models. Generalists, for example, are trying to add specialty centers within their business to appeal to emerging new market segments. Specialists are trying to add lines to make their small businesses more recession proof and less vulnerable to market changes.

In addition to these technological, social and economic factors, some additional changes are occurring near the generalist end of the distributor continuum. Generalists have transactional sales that are roughly defined as the sales of commodity product in very simplistic buy-sell transactions. These transactions are being impacted by three primary forces:

1. electronic business transactions,

2. big-box retailers such as Home Depot, or Wal-Mart, and
3. C-parts consolidators.

Electronic business is not going to replace distributors, but it is changing the way they do business. Manufacturers use the Internet as part of a multitiered approach to marketing, whereas distributors use it to provide 24/7 customer service. In the heating, ventilating, and air conditioning (HVAC) industry, for example, many leading manufacturers and channels are using electronic media. Rheem Manufacturing provides information to both consumers and channel partners through its Web site, which is designed to guide the respective customer to pages designed specifically for each audience. Parker Hannifin has a portal strategy to address different needs; for channel partners, the site provides the ability to check order status, track package shipments, search the master catalog, place orders, and check current invoices.[1]

Big-box retailers have taken over a great deal of small contractor business from generalist distributors. When small contractors went to the local distributor they were regarded as "C" customers and given very little discount, inventory programs, or service support programs. But big-box retailers offer more outlets at more convenient locations with competitive pricing no matter the purchasing volume. Thus, small contractors found it easier, more convenient, and more cost effective to go to the big-box retailers to acquire primary parts and supply items for their repair services. Big-box retailers also had extended hours, weekend hours, and other convenience advantages that attracted small contractors. Many big-box retailers are now experimenting with contractor centers, express lines for contractors, and the extension of credit to small contractors.

A third force is C-parts consolidators. A consolidator will approach a facility that is purchasing A, B, and C parts and offer to handle the C-part procurement on an outsourcing basis. The desired result to the manufacturer is a much lower total acquisition cost of C-parts. A consolidator provides all the parts, manages them to the point of use on the manufacturing floor, and maintains a consistent price for the part. The soft costs of purchasing time, inspection, central stores, and internal parts distribution are eliminated.

Although this approach is primarily a soft-cost saving, it is very appealing to manufacturers struggling to lower overall manufacturing costs. Generalist distributors are trying to fight back by providing increased value to transactional purchases. Increasing value to a transactional purchase is a difficult task and is changing the fundamental business model of generalist distribution.

Whatever business shifts distributors are contemplating, three things are very clear. Distributors must

1. shift their traditional business models,
2. find new ways to create value, and
3. identify emerging market segments more quickly.

The distributors who survive these changes will emerge as better business planners, marketers, and sales organizations. Insightful manufacturers will seize this opportunity to help distributors evolve and be rewarded in the future with a team of capable and loyal distributors.

Reflection Point

How do I help my distributors acquire new skills, evolve, and thrive through change?

▶ Do I have Internet strategy for dealing with my channel?

Manufacturing and Distributor Differences

Understanding distributors means understanding the primary differences between manufacturing and distribution business operations. See Figure 9-1 for an overview of the key differences between manufacturers and distributors, especially privately held distributors.

The first difference is how manufacturers and distributors define and execute the sales function. A manufacturer views sales as a consultative process including lead generation, qualifying, presenting, building consensus, handling objections, and gaining customer commitment. A distributor views sales as relationship building and order fulfillment. The manufacturer believes sales to be the strategic activity of account qualification and persuasion.

These opposing viewpoints become clear to the manufacturer when making sales calls with the distributor's sales person. When a customer asks for a specific brand of product, distributor salespeople will either

	Manufacturers	Distributors
Financial Drivers	▪ Revenue and Budgets ▪ Market Penetration ▪ Profit ▪ ROI ▪ Stock Price	▪ Sales ▪ Gross Margin ▪ Cash Flow ▪ Earns and Turns ▪ Owners' Risks
Marketing	▪ Target Market Segments ▪ Positioning	▪ Accounts
Competitive Advantages	▪ Product, Quality, Features ▪ Warranty	▪ Account Relationships ▪ Stock Levels
Time Horizon	▪ 1, 2, and 5 years	▪ Tomorrow, this month
Planning Output	▪ Team Commitment	▪ Action Timetable

Sales	▪ Qualification and
	  Persuasive
	  Presentation
		▪ Take Orders, Build
		  Relationships, and
		  Explain Promotions

Figure 9-1. Business differences between manufacturers and distributors

take the order or say they don't carry that particular product. Manufacturers see the same customer request as a golden opportunity to make a conversion sale and grow market share. Manufacturers can't understand why the distributor doesn't share that simple logic. The distributor, on the other hand, can't imagine telling customers to change their requirements for the sake of a single sale. The distributor values the long-term relationship much more than the short-term reward of one conversion sale. These differing points of view can lead to frustration, failed expectations and erosion of the working relationship between the manufacturer and distributor.

A second dichotomous discussion occurs when a manufacturer and a distributor discuss competitive advantages. The manufacturer believes competitive advantage comes from product quality, features, and programs such as warranty and technical support. A distributor believes that a competitive advantage comes from building relationships, product availability, convenient location, and price. The manufacturer often attempts to convert the distributor to its point of view with literature and promotions. Such attempts meet with limited success because they don't address the underlying differences and they don't recognize the fact that for many distributor customers, the competitive advantage is the relationship more than the product.

Another critical difference is the way manufacturers and distributors see the marketplace. Manufacturers tend to focus on markets, market segments, niches, and target markets, while distributors focus on accounts. Distributors rarely know—much less care—what target market an account is in. They simply see it as an account with the potential to buy a certain product. Manufacturers define their marketing plans and programs around target-market segments. These differences often lead distributors to believe that manufacturer's plans, strategies, and programs do not apply to them and their territories.

The financial drivers of a manufacturing company and their employees are very different than those of a distributorship. A manufacturer is driven by forecast revenue, budgets, market penetration, strategic execution, and, of course, return to the stockholders. The employees are rewarded by a salary and, in some small part, a bonus tied to the company's ability to achieve goals. Distributors pay close attention to cash flow, sales, margin, receivables, and inventory position. Small distributors, in particular, have financial goals that are much closer to balancing a checkbook. Cash flow is normally a distributor's most critical financial metric, while manufacturers focus on their stock price or price-to-earnings ratio.

A distributorship is also very aware of the owner's personal and business risk and how that risk relates to each sale, business decision, and activity. In short, the distributor does not enjoy the long-term cash buffer or institutional inertia that can keep a manufacturing operation alive through a few years of variable performance.

Another critical difference is time horizons. A manufacturer's planning time horizon is typically one, two, and five years. A distributor's planning horizon is now, this week, this month, and this quarter. Actions and decisions revolve around short-term goals and growing customer relationships. The planning function of a manufacturing company includes marketing research reports, field reports, and market intelligence. A lengthy document is produced that contains hundreds of pages of complex strategies, technical details, and several appendixes.

The distributor's plan, if one exists, is usually based on the opinion of a few key people and is a couple of pages long; it is more tactical than strategic and is centered on an action plan: who will do what by when. Most distributors are still gaining experience as planners. However, the clarity and action orientation of these plans can lead to more direct implementation than the megaplans produced by manufacturers. The consequences of these time and planning differences make the manufacturers appear large, slow, philosophical, and unresponsive compared with the distributor's commitment to daily customer care.

In the end, the differences between manufacturer and distributor business operations give rise to misunderstanding, ill-fitting marketing programs, and little trust. The solution isn't to attempt to change the differences but to accommodate them in manufacturer and distributor business plans.

Reflection Piont	**Do I have a clear understanding of the differences between manufacturer and distributor business operations?**
	▶ What are the top three financial drivers of my key distributors?
	▶ How well do I translate marketing and sales plans into action plans for my distributors?

Changes in Distributor Operations

The forces of market, technical, social, and economic change discussed in this chapter have led to two new conditions:

1. Distributors must change their basic business models to survive.
2. Manufacturer and distributor relationships must be recast to accommodate the changes.

Initial changes to distributor business models are underway. Distributors are becoming more financially sophisticated. Previously, distributors evaluated product lines on gross margin and annual inventory turns; today they are using more sophisticated measures such as Gross Margin Return on Inventory Investment or GMROII. This ratio compares gross margin obtained to inventory carrying costs allowing the distributor to evaluate return on inventory investment for each product line they carry; it is calculated by dividing total annual gross profit of the product line by the product line's average monthly inventory investment at cost.

A second change is the increasing complexity of the distributor business model. Generalists are incorporating specialty operations, and specialists are adding lines and markets to increase revenue. For distributors to change their business models, they must acquire new business and management skills to run their much more complex multifaceted business.

A third area of change is in distributors sales operations. The days of being an order taker are dying, and the switch to consultative selling has begun. Manufacturers are assisting and educating distributors in the process. The early results are mixed, but the necessity of the change is no longer in question. The amount and rate of these changes is unprecedented and unsettling for manufacturers who rely on distributors to execute their sales and marketing plans.

Reflection Point

How are the business models of my distributors changing?
▶ What am I doing to help them evolve?

Changes in Manufacturer and Distributor Relationships

The biggest change in the distributor/manufacturer relationship is the sharing of business functions. Traditionally, these functions had been solely assigned to one or the other. For example, extending local credit used to be the sole responsibility of the distributor. Today, many manufacturers have created lease programs to help distributors increase sales and create an aftermarket for used equipment. A case in point is the Manitowoc Ice Machine Division of the Manitowoc Company. The fastest-growing dealer segment in the early 1990s for ice machines was *leasing dealers*. This market was opened up because the Manitowoc Company established a leasing program for dealers that their distributors could use to enhance sales. The credit function was consequently shared between the manufacturer and distributor.

Local inventory is another function that manufacturers typically left to the distributor. However, duplication of inventory at the manufacturer and distributor locations drives up the cost to the end user. As a result, manufacturers and distributors developed drop-ship programs, on-site inventory programs, and regional warehousing options.

The Trane Company's best parts distributor center utilizes an aggressive on-site inventory program for its dealers. Parts are stored at customer locations until needed. When a part is removed from the inventory, a sale is made. Inventory is now a shared function.

It only makes sense that if traditional functions are shared, compensation for the execution of the function should also be shared. Consequently, manufacturers and distributors are renegotiating their contracts based on value provided to the end user. Optimizing end-user satisfaction is the goal of the new manufacturer and distributor partnership and a requirement of global competition.

> **Reflection Point**
>
> **What are the key friction points I have with my distributors?**
> ▶ Could those areas benefit from redesigning responsibilities in the relationship?
> ▶ Could the responsibility for specific functions be shifted or shared?

Strategic Implications for Manufacturers

Manufacturers must assess their distributor's strategic implementation capabilities. Their assessment of these capabilities will influence what the type, level, and sophistication of marketing strategy they initiate. Below are five strategic considerations that will affect implementation success with distributions.

Make Strategies Simple. Manufacturers should develop simple and straightforward marketing strategies. It takes roughly one year for a channel to learn what suppliers want it to do and a second year to become proficient. Complex strategies lengthen these time frames and decrease the percentage of distributors who can execute a plan.

Demonstrate Advantages. Manufacturers should not use an intangible advantage as the core element in their distributor sales strategies. The most successful strategy a manufacturer can use with a distributor is a visual differentiation that is clear and demonstrable. A product with a demonstrable or visible difference is critical to the distributor's sale. Although distributors are evolving from order taking to consultative selling, they still need help making the transition.

Demonstrable or visual differences are easy to teach, easy to learn, and easy to use with customers. They help distributor salespeople become more comfortable, knowledgeable, and influential in front of their customers.

A clear example of these two principles is evident in the historic rise of Manitowoc Ice Machines over a 15-year period. When Manitowoc entered the business of making ice machines, they did it with a quality product that had a very simple difference from other ice machines. The ice machine used gravity to harvest the ice. All competitive models used complex mechanical systems to harvest the ice. Manitowoc's sales claim was simple and visual, allowing it to grow into the market leader.

The interesting part of this story occurred after the patent period ran out. Manitowoc, at that time, changed its strategy to "product, quality, and service," which is a highly complex and intangible approach. This strategy led to a drop in market share. Three years later, Manitowoc reinvented its competitive advantage by becoming the only self-cleaning, self-sanitizing ice machine on the market. This new, clear, and simple strategy created an increase in market share beyond their market share apex three years prior.

The lesson is clear; your strategy should be visibly different from the competition so your distributors can confidentially show their customers why you are the better choice.

Be Consistent. A third strategic imperative is consistency. As noted earlier, channel partners require a great deal of time to learn and execute a strategy in the marketplace. If you change your strategy frequently, you are continuously retraining and ultimately confusing your distributors. Your strategy gets muddier and muddled as it is communicated through your channel to the end user. If you change your strategy frequently through a large distribution network, you have diminished your chance for crisp execution.

Strategies succeed or fail based on the quality of the implementation effort, as evidenced by a conversation between two market managers. After the first one said, "Here's my strategy ..." the other replied, "That is a terrible strategy." To which the first manager calmly replied, "That doesn't mean it won't work." His reasoning was simple: a mediocre strategy well implemented will beat a poorly implemented great strategy every time. A simple, visible, and consistent strategy has the best chance to be well implemented.

Choose Appropriate Levels of "Push" or "Pull" Selling. The fourth strategic imperative is selecting the appropriate amount of push or pull selling for your channel. If you supply a minor or secondary product line, your distribution channel requires a predominantly *pull* marketing strategy, which is based on building end-user demand through communications to drive end users to your distributors. Major brands such as Coca-Cola, Dial, Kohler, or Honeywell use a pull strategy.

A major product line supplier can use a *push* strategy to drive its product through the channel with high sales exposure and sales effort. If you are using a push strategy, a strong component is product training, application training, and sales training so distributors have the tools they need to succeed.

Offer Translation. A fifth strategic imperative is translating the manufacturer's national marketing plan into a distributor sales call. Most manufacturers make the mistake of unveiling their annual marketing plans and expecting distributors to interpret the plan correctly and create perfectly consistent sales plans and sales calls. Manufacturers' plans have a much higher probability of proper execution if the job of developing distributor sales calls is assigned to a team and then released to the regional management team for a strong follow-through training program that includes role-playing, as well as a measurement-and-reward follow-up effort.

This linkage, or lack thereof, is usually one of the critical breakdown points in strategic implementation when working through distributors.

In summary, the strategies that work best with distributors contain (1) simplicity, (2) a clear, visible, and demonstrable difference, (3) consistency over time, (4) an appropriate level of push or pull selling, and (5) a translation of the manufacturer's sales and marketing plan into a distributor's sales call. Invest 90% of your effort on implementing your channel strategy because quality implementation has more impact on your success or failure than any other variable.

How have I made my competitive advantage clear and visible for my distributors?

▶ Can they put it in their customers' hands or on the counter?

▶ Have I determined the appropriate level of push and pull selling?

Key Points

▶ Distributor operations are changing at an unprecedented rate due to technical, social, and economic forces. Distributors must learn to adapt, change, and manage more complex business models.

▶ Manufacturer and distributor relationships are becoming more complex as they share functional responsibility for sales execution.

▶ Manufacturers must develop sales and marketing strategies that fit their distributors' capabilities and aggressively assist them during implementation.

Notes

1. John R. Hall, "Transacting Business Over the Internet," *Air Conditioning, Heating & Refrigeration News*, 24 March 2003, p. 17.

Chapter 10

ESTABLISHING MUTUAL PERFORMANCE EXPECTATIONS

The importance of strategy execution was emphasized in the previous chapter. A great strategy will not be successful if it is poorly implemented. That's why the remainder of this book is devoted to improving the ongoing relationship between a supplier and its channel partners. This chapter addresses Stage V of the channel design process, as shown in Figure 10-1.

Traditional Role Expectations

A distributor's primary responsibilities have been to sell and promote the manufacturer's products in a defined geographic region, extend credit, and carry appropriate levels of stock. (Refer to Figure 10-2 for manufacturer and distributor functions.) These traditional and clear-cut roles had little annual variability or discussion except for the annual sales forecast. During forecast review meetings, the manufacturer would tell the distributor what its sales forecast should be for the coming year. The distributor would usually counter with a very different number. A lively discussion would ensue. The result was always a negotiated forecast and often bitter feelings.

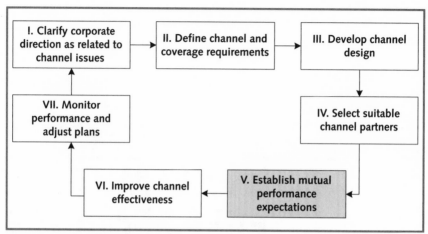

Figure 10-1. Stage V of channel redesign

This simplistic arm-wrestling approach has given way to a more comprehensive business discussion. These discussions are a sharing of the business plans by both manufacturers and distributors. The manufacturer usually takes the lead by sharing detailed plans for the coming year, product improvements, quality improvements, process improvements, new products, sales programs, incentives, cooperative promotional programs, and sales goals by product and market. After

Manufacturer's Role	Distributor's Role
• Production of a consistent quality product • Technical support • Sales and technical training • Development of new products • Market research • Communication and sales program • Warranty and returns policies • Sales leads • Parts and service training • Timely delivery • Pricing • Contract defining relationship • Sales call assistance • Brand marketing	• Local stocking of product and parts • Technical support • Local market information • Local creditor lease programs • Payment of bills • Sales forecasts • Local marketing

Figure 10-2. Traditional roles of manufacturers and distributors

hearing the manufacturer's plan, distributors develop and share their plans for the coming year. Their sales plans include their view of local market conditions, key operational changes, and their sales forecast by product and market.

Although these types of discussions ultimately lead to the same point as those previously described—a sales forecast by product and market—today's negotiations are now a shared, informative, and collaborative effort. Each party has the opportunity to alter its plans based on the information shared.

Against this backdrop of increased information exchange between manufacturers and distributors, this chapter contains:

- ▶ requirements for manufacturer business plans,
- ▶ requirements for distributor business plans,
- ▶ example distributor profiles to establish distributor performance matrics, and
- ▶ an example market penetration index to compare distributor performance.

Manufacturer Plans

The manufacturer's business plan is generally announced annually to distributors via an annual meeting, a national broadcast event, distributed by the local regional managers or mailed out with collateral materials and follow-up plans. The method of the announcement of the manufacturer's annual plan to the distribution channel depends on the manufacturer's budget, the relative importance of the manufacturer's line to the distributors, and the amount of change in the plan. The choice is also heavily influenced by tradition, that is, how it has been done in the past.

The amount of planning, energy, and money the manufacturer invests in the communication of the annual plan indicates the relative importance of the plan. A list of subjects normally covered by the manufacturer's plan for distributors is seen in Figure 10-3.

After the manufacturer has presented the key elements of its plan, time is usually set aside for a question-and-answer session. If the plan is presented at an annual meeting, a variety of other activities are included, such as an awards dinner, a distributor roundtable

Section 1—Business Overview
▶ A review of last year's sales results
▶ Business plan overview
▶ Competition and market situations
▶ Channel overview
▶ Marketing and sales strategy
▶ Sales goals

Section 2—Product Overview
▶ New products
▶ Product updates
▶ Quality improvements
▶ Manufacturing overview
▶ Technical trends

Section 3—Distributor Programs Overview
▶ Sales programs
▶ Advertising and publicity
▶ Literature
▶ Trade shows
▶ Cooperative advertising
▶ Sales contests & incentive programs
▶ Training programs
▶ Specific issues:
    National accounts
    E-business
    Buying groups

Section 4—Sales Forecast
▶ By product
▶ By market
▶ Penetration index

Figure 10-3. Manufacturer's business plan outline

input session, outside speakers, social outings, or other events. If the meeting is at or near the manufacturer's location, it often includes factory tours and is an excellent opportunity to incorporate in-depth product training, technical training, and skill development training.

When manufacturers prepare their annual distributor meetings, they adhere to three basic ground rules:

1. Make it fun.
2. Make it specific.
3. Make it honest.

To make it fun, schedule the meeting in an interesting travel destination and make each session high energy, high motivation, and high involvement.

Make it specific by talking in the "language" of the distributor. Manufacturers tend to speak in generalities such as market segments, niches, and positions. Distributors think in specifics such as products, sales, and accounts. Distributors want specific information on what is going to happen, when it's going to happen, and what role the distributor will play in making it happen.

Finally, distributors want honest and accurate information. Overly optimistic or pessimistic manufacturer's projections can harm a distributor's "hand-to-mouth" business operation if used as a basis for distributor business planning.

Distributor Plans

After the manufacturer's plan has been presented, the manufacturer's regional sales managers schedule meetings with their distributors to listen to their plans for the coming year. The emphasis in these planning sessions is to assure that distributor plans align with the manufacturer's direction, review forecasts, and discuss problems and opportunities.

Formal written business planning is a relatively new concept for many distributors. For years, smaller distributors didn't plan because little changed from year to year. Distributors were required only to write simple financial plans for their banker and note any major operational changes for the coming year.

Many distributors fought the idea of formal business plans, claiming it wouldn't be worth the effort. The following is a sample of typical distributors' arguments against planning. "We are meeting our goals now." "Who has the time?" "We plan informally now." "Plans are written and then forgotten anyway." "Things change too quickly." "Our forecast depends on a few key customers anyway." Unspoken resistance also came from unfamiliarity with the task and not knowing how to get started.

Why should a distributor plan? The overriding reason is because of the increased rate of change in their business from year to year. The specific business arguments for distributor planning are:

1. It sets the primary direction for the distributorship;
2. It establishes goals, both financial and key activities;
3. It enables measurement of key activities and sales goals;
4. It prioritizes and coordinates daily decisions; and
5. Most important, it increases the probability of business success.

Simply put, companies with business plans outperform those who don't have plans. What types of planning efforts have been most successful for distributors? Ideas to initiate or improve distributor planning follow.

Keep it simple. Distributors are closer to firefighters than microchip process engineers. Distributor plans should be simple and clear enough to operate under the normally chaotic conditions of responding to daily and immediate customer problems and requests.

Make plans measurable. If a goal isn't clear and measurable, it shouldn't be in a distributor's plan. All key actions should be directly related to goal achievement. Goals should be focused on sales growth, account and market penetration, introducing new products or increasing end-user customer satisfaction levels, not on beating the competition. Distributors tend to be reactive and overly competitive. Consequently they put too much energy into beating the competition rather than planning their own future. Competitive reaction is particularly dangerous when developing pricing strategies.

Include long-term goals. Planning—in small distributorships particularly—has been aimed at short-term goals and activities. Distributors don't take a longer view because they are focused on cash flow and daily sales. Financial goals drive short-term success but usually at the expense of long-term market position and overall capability.

Develop a monitoring system. Distributor plans run a high risk of being put away forever as the rush of daily activity overtakes distributor operations. If distributor plans don't force monthly monitoring and review, they will be written, filed and quickly forgotten.

Communicate the plan. Training and communication must be provided to the entire organization before success can be expected. The majority of distributors are small businesses, and every employee must understand and contribute for planned success to be achieved.

How should a distributor get started? The easiest way to begin distributor planning is to start small and simply by addressing these three basic questions:

1. "Where do we want to go?"
2. "Who will we serve?"
3. "How will we be the best?"

Answers to these questions will form the fundamental mission of the distributor's business. Begin the annual planning process by asking, "What do we need to do this year to get started?" Manufacturers can act as a catalyst and play an important role by encouraging distributors to become more competent business planners, more sophisticated financially, and more strategic in the areas of marketing and sales. The reward for the manufacturer is a stronger and more loyal channel partner.

As distributors get increasingly comfortable with business planning, more complex and strategic planning outlines can be attempted. More detailed distribution business plans should include their strengths, weaknesses, threats and opportunities, a brief strategy, sales and marketing activities, a sales forecast by product and market, and an action timetable. See Figure 10-4 for an example of a distributor business plan outline.

Overview of Distributor Operations

Sales Review of Last Year's Sales Results
Overall sales $
- ► By products
- ► By markets
- ► Penetration index or market share estimates

Figure 10-4. Distributor business plan outline (continued on next page)

▶ Primary reasons for these results

Business analysis

▶ Strengths

▶ Weaknesses

▶ Threats

▶ Opportunities

Current situation

▶ Markets

▶ Competition

▶ Capabilities

▶ Key accounts

▶ Branches (if applicable)

Goals

▶ Sales goals for next year

▶ Operational goals

▶ Qualitative goals

Sales Strategy

Sales activities

▶ Sales coverage

▶ Promotions

▶ Events

▶ Direct mail

▶ Market/product emphasis

▶ Incentive programs

Sales forecast detail

▶ Products

▶ Markets

▶ Key accounts

▶ Branches

Action timetable

▶ Who, what, when

Figure 10-4. Distributor business plan outline (continued)

Although distributors rarely share the entirety of their plans with a manufacturer, they should share the product and market aspects of their business that directly affect the manufacturer's product line—as well as major internal, structural, or operational changes that will impact their ability to execute sales, promotion, stocking, and support responsibilities. Shared planning meetings should produce a clear understanding of assumptions, strategies, activities, and sales forecasts. The action plan enables the manufacturer and distributor to monitor the key activities throughout the year and make necessary adjustments to achieve the desired sales goals.

Distributors are facing more competition than ever and experiencing the pain of dead stock and overstocked products. These facts are leading them to do more and better forecasting by collaborating with channel partners rather than simply relying on past usage. Collaborative planning forecasting and replenishment (CPFR or just collaborative forecasting) is the process of distributors linking downstream with customers (and perhaps upstream with suppliers) to predict the future usage of products.

According to Jon Schreibfeder in *Progressive Distributor*

> Advances in electronic commerce have facilitated better communications between computer systems that has resulted in the development of electronic CPFR systems. Many distribution systems can now be set to receive inventory requirement information from their customer's scheduling and production software. These requirements are considered in the distributor's demand forecast calculations.[1]

Distributor Profiles

Manufacturers are constantly trying to determine why some distributors outperform others. One method of identifying the critical performance differences is to build a profile of the most successful distributors in the channel. Building a distributor profile is relatively easy if you follow this five-step process.

1. Select the top 10 percent of the distributors in your channel based on market share performance.
2. List the attributes that best describe each of these distributors.
3. Identify the attributes that appear on a majority of the lists.
4. Condense the attribute list to the five or six that appear most frequently.

5. Review the list with selected distributors and regional sales managers for their reaction and validation.

To further validate your attribute list, rank order all the distributors in the channel by market share and score them against the distributor profile characteristics from one to five. If top performing distributors score highest on the profile and the poor performing distributors score lower on the profile, you have created a reasonably valid distributor profile. A final way to validate your profile is to go to downstream channel members and ask them which distributors they prefer and why. If their answers match or reinforce your distributor profile, you have confirmed profile validity.

The distributor profile has two primary uses. First, it can be used to select or cancel distributors. As such it can be used to refine the "ideal candidate" template described in an earlier stage of the channel design process. (See Figure 8-2 in Chapter 8.) Second, it can be used to coach distributors. The profile helps identify where performance may be improved. Figure 10-5 presents a distributor profile for XYZ manufacturer, where XYZ supplies a *major* line for the distributor (as defined in Figure 8-4 in Chapter 8). A distributor is rated from five to one for each attribute to develop an overall profile. If a distributor scores a rating of one or two in any category, that category

	Rating Excellent				Poor
	5	4	3	2	1
Enthusiastic owner support					
Dedicated XYZ champion					
High quality technical people					
XYZ products are their competitive edge					
Focused on our market					
Sell systems, not boxes					
Effective internal operating systems and management					

Figure 10-5. Distributor profile (see notes on next page)

Key Attributes of a Successful XYZ Distributor Defined

Enthusiastic owner support

Owner believes and promotes both XYZ product line and strategy that is crucial to their success in the market place. Also places XYZ as 1 of their top 3 product lines. Knows where XYZ sales are relative to whole distributor sales and factors causing it. Always shares all XYZ information received at meetings or through memos. Promotes support tools and XYZ capabilities on a continuous basis.

Dedicated XYZ specialist

An individual appointed as the "XYZ Product Line Manager"

High-quality technical people

Regularly sends sales people to XYZ training schools. Understands the need for technical education and may at times provide or require supplemental courses for career development. Agrees that a technical background is a key factor to successful XYZ product application and system designs.

XYZ products are their competitive edge, important to their success

Uses the XYZ name to convey quality and performance to set themselves apart from competitive distributors.

Focused on our markets

Understands and channels sales efforts to capture available original equipment manufacturers and industries, providing replacement business in the future. Does not depend on market growth for XYZ sales growth, is proactive on displacing competitors products and enhancing applications.

Sells systems, not boxes

Does not sell products from a catalog or by simply cross-referencing. Reviews each application as a new opportunity. Maximizes these opportunities with a combination of XYZ product sales with other components.

Effective internal operating systems and management

Has in place office management systems to efficiently produce, monitor, and supply orders, invoices, inventory, and shipments. Also stays progressive with office technology equipment and communications.

becomes an area for potential improvement. Valid profiles provide an excellent guideline for selecting, managing, and canceling distributors in your network.

> **Reflection Point**
>
> **How does my distributor profile compare to the examples in Figure 10-5 and 8-2?**
> ▸ How well does my distributor profile predict sales success?
> ▸ How will I use my distributor profile to improve individual distributor performance?

How Distributors Evaluate Manufacturers

Long before distributors represent a manufacturer, they are aware of the manufacturer's products and reputation in the market. In many cases, they have competed against them. At some point, the distributor and the manufacturer get together to explore a partnership. During that process the distributor gets a close look at the manufacturer's products, capabilities, and policies.

Once distributors acquire the manufacturer's line, they begin to interact on a more personal and consistent basis. Through these interactions, they get to know the manufacturer's ability and willingness to respond to customer problems. Willingness and ability translate into, "They are easy to do business with." or "Boy, are they ever messed up!"

The opinion is primarily based on the courtesy and problem resolution provided by the manufacturer during daily phone calls. Distributors call for help with inventory, product support, training, literature, product problems, warranty issues, or scrapage problems. The manufacturer is either friendly and easy to work with or difficult.

> **Reflection Point**
>
> **How do my distributors rate my products, policies and ease of doing business?**
> ▸ How does this impact my downstream channel members and end users?

The distributor's opinion of the manufacturer impacts how aggressively they will work to resolve customer problems. In short, the manufacturer's reputation with the distributor becomes the manufacturer's reputation with downstream channel members and end users.

Penetration Index

A penetration index is an indicator of local market sales penetration. A penetration index permits the comparison of distributor sales performance independent of local market size. It makes possible a reasonably fair comparison between a large city distributor (e.g., in Chicago), and a smaller market distributor (e.g., in Albuquerque). The critical element in developing a penetration index is finding an accurate yardstick to measure market size. An example makes this concept easier to understand. If you are selling toothpaste, a penetration index yardstick could be population. A distributor in a city of ten million people should sell ten times more toothpaste than a distributor in a city of one million people. The concept is relatively simple.

However, industrial products usually don't follow population numbers, so finding a valid yardstick becomes the first challenge in constructing a useful penetration index. For example, a maintenance, repair, and operations (MRO) supplier could base its penetration index yardstick on the number and size of manufacturing facilities within a given North American Industry Classification System (NAICS)—previously referred to as the Standard Industrial Classification (SIC) code.

Yardsticks can be refined by the addition of other variables over time. Once refined and validated, the penetration index becomes a valuable tool to monitor distributor performance. When a distributor's penetration index drops below company average, check its profile ratings to see which activities or attributes need attention.

Reflection Point

How do I compare distributor performance from one market to another?
▶ What is my yardstick for PI comparison?
▶ Is my yardstick fair and equitable?

The penetration index is used primarily as an indicator. Manufacturers establish a penetration index average based on all their distributors' sales. Each distributor above the average is said to be above the 100 percent penetration index (PI), and distributors who fall below average have a PI below 100 percent. Distributors who achieve a PI above 100 percent may receive recognition awards or incentives at the end of the year. Distributors who fall below 90 percent PI are usually put on notice for improvement or potential cancellation.

The penetration index is a valuable indicator for evaluating distributor results. It may also be useful to refer back to the discussion of market share in Chapter 5, where the impacts of product fit, distribution availability, and win rate on territory analysis are presented.[2]

Key Points

▶ The amount of change and complexity in channels of distribution has led to an increased level of shared information and coordination of activities between manufacturers and distributors.

▶ Both manufacturers and distributors are managing more complex businesses.

▶ Manufacturers should develop distributor penetration indexes and profiles to better monitor and manage distributor performance.

▶ Distributors are challenged to become better business planners, more financially savvy, and more professional in their approach to sales and target marketing. Manufacturers can play a valuable role by encouraging and training their distributors to meet these challenges.

Notes

1. Jon Schreibfeder, "Reduce Inventory with Collaborative Forecasting," *Progressive Distributor*, March/April 2001, pp. 5 ff.

2. Chapter 5 of this book contains information on providing channel and coverage requirements from a strategic perspective. As such, the distributor profile and market share calculations were presented as tools of channel design. Although they link to the profile and penetration index in this chapter, the emphasis here is working with an existing channel. It may be useful to compare and contrast the techniques for your usage as appropriate.

Chapter 11

IMPROVING CHANNEL EFFECTIVENESS

Once mutual performance expectations are set and plans developed, the manufacturer's task shifts to helping distributors and other channel partners attain their objectives and implement their plans. This is stage VI in the channel design process as shown in Figure 11-1.

This chapter will focus on helping distributors become more effective in selling your products. It's worth noting that these techniques will work best if you are using a push strategy with a product line of major or secondary importance to the distributor. Manufacturers of products of minor importance to distributors may be best served by exploring pull sales strategies—or encouraging distributors to cross sell their products when they are selling a complementary major product—or working with complementary manufacturers in a bundling strategy.

Six Components to Improve Channel Effectiveness

In this chapter, you'll read about the primary methods that manufacturers employ to improve distributor performance. In particular, the

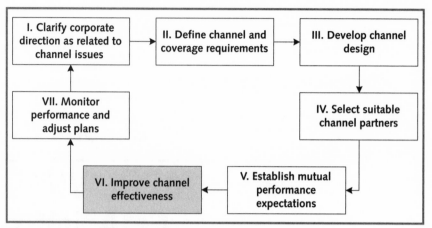

Figure 11-1. Stage VI of channel redesign

following six concepts will be discussed in depth:

1. Sell all levels of the distributorship on the value and financial return achievable by successfully implementing the manufacturer's plan.

2. Select a product champion or product-line specialist to become the manufacturer's key contact person to facilitate program implementation and coordination of activities.

3. Coach the product champion or product line specialist in all aspects of selling. The product-line specialist should become the most skilled and productive salesperson for the manufacturer's product line, as well as an inventory specialist, a promotion expert, and the spearhead of the manufacturer's implementation efforts.

4. Train all distributor salespeople, customer contact personnel and down-line channel members on relevant products, markets, applications, service, and sales procedures. Everyone with customer contact responsibility at the distributorship should be able to handle customer contact with a feeling of confidence and competence.

5. Provide guidance on promotion and advertising efforts including co-op programs, literature, trade shows, promotions, special incentives, and events.

6. Become a business consultant and financial advisor to the distributor owner.

Selling to Your Distributors

Before a manufacturer can help a distributor become more successful, the manufacturer must build a strong personal relationship with all levels of the distributorship and then sell them on the value of its products and programs. To do this, manufacturers should have a qualified and talented regional sales manager (RSM) calling on the distributor with a multilevel and multifaceted sales plan.

The plan should include the identification of the key players, sales goals by product and market, a general strategy, a sales call schedule, and specific issues to be accomplished or resolved during the year. Some issues to consider are: train appropriate personnel on markets, technology, products, systems, and selling skills; sales promotion activity plan; coaching for your product champion or specialist; assistance to be provided to key salespeople and customer service personnel; coordination of literature, sales promotions, policies, product samples, field directives, product warranties, returns, and scrapage; and finally, consultations with the distributor's owner on critical business challenges and opportunities. The sales plan for calling on a distributor is extremely complex and requires a variety of skills to implement.

Regional Sales Manager

RSMs must possess the following 10 skill sets to successfully call on and work through distributors:

1. Sell the manufacturers' products and programs to the owner, the middle managers and functional titles such as sales, customer service, and purchasing.
2. Present training and education on sales, customer service, products, markets, technical knowledge, and procedures.
3. Provide assistance on sales calls.
4. Coach the product specialist or champion over an extended period of time.
5. Assist in sales promotions and sales incentive programs.
6. Build customer relationships with all channel members and help the distributor build relationships.
7. Organize the channel to minimize conflict and competition with down-stream customers.
8. Update distributor information, literature, and trade shows.

9. Coordinate warranty, return, and all other policies.
10. Consult on financial matters—being sensitive to the distributor's financial imperatives—and assist the owner in business planning.

Finding a fully qualified RSM is difficult because so much is required from one person. Hiring a RSM normally becomes an exercise in prioritizing and compromising on the skill sets required.

Distributor Resale Motivations

Distributors do not buy a product because it is the best in its class or because it has highly desirable features; they buy it to resell it. Their primary business function is selling. Manufacturers should not attempt to sell their products' qualities to distributors; manufacturers should be selling programs that enable ease of resale and at high margins, increased commissions, and enhanced customer relationships.

The different levels within the distributorship have different resale motivations. The distributorship owners are most interested in profitability and the financial requirements for carrying the line. The mid-managers are most interested in the effect a product line has on employee enthusiasm, customer retention, and compatibility with operating systems. The counter people, salespeople, and purchasing and technical support personnel are most interested in product quality, ease of resale, ease of policy execution, technical support programs, and commissions.

It is critical for the manufacturer's program to appeal to the different levels of distributor personnel, department objectives, and the organization's most critical goals. See Figure 11-2 for an outline of a manufacturer's sales plan for calling on a distributor.

Functional Discounts

Manufacturers regularly offer price incentives for distributors if they buy in quantity. The assumption had always been that if the distributors bought a lot of the product, they would have to sell it. However, this traditional sales strategy focuses on selling *to* the distributor rather than *through* the distributor. It is not an effective way to build channel relationships or increase end-user value, and it can be very disruptive to end-market pricing.

Identification

Name _____

Location _____

Branches _____

Owner _____

Goals

Last Year's Sales by   Products _____

Markets _____

Branches _____

This Year's Sales Goals by   Products _____

Markets _____

Branches _____

Strategy

Brief and General Statement of Strategy

_____

_____

_____

Potential Actions

Developing new and multilevel relationships

Training   Product

Technology

Sales

Service

Give guidance on promotions, advertising, direct mail, e-mail, and events

Advise and administer co-op fund

Develop product line champion

Provide sales assistance

Assist owner in business planning and monitoring

Provide routine functions: information and literature updating

        Administer: Promotional programs

Warranty and returns

Policy conflict resolution

Calling Schdule

Date	Objective	Contact
_____	_____	_____
_____	_____	_____

Figure 11-2. Annual sales plan for calling on distributors

A better approach to drive market share sales goals is to offer functional discount programs based on distributor's participation in marketing, sales and promotion programs. (See Chapters 1, 4, and 6 for additional information on functional discounts.) Functional discount programs assign a discount or financial value to activities, such as trade show participation, direct mail campaigns, counter displays, promotional participation, attending technical or sales training sessions, passing competency tests, and lead follow-up campaigns. Functional discounts reward the activity and effort that manufacturers require for their products and programs to succeed.

Selecting a Product Champion or Product-Line Specialist

Why should a manufacturer develop a product champion or product-

Reflection Point

> **How well do our RSMs sell our programs for profit to our distributors?**
> ▶ Do we address concerns at all levels of the distributorship?
> ▶ Do we understand that we are not selling a "box," but rather the ability to earn margin?
> ▶ Do we recognize and reward our distributors for the market development functions they perform?

line specialist strategy? The reason is simple: manufacturers cannot convince every distributor employee, from owner through warehouse personnel, of the values of their product line. Manufacturers need one point person within each distributorship to act as a primary contact and sales expert. Manufacturers, through their RSMs, select a product champion who can become an enthusiastic link to focus and maximize influence in each distributorship.

Who should be your champion? Manufacturers vie for influence with the top sales talent in distributorships, so it is likely the best salespeople are already dedicated to a major product line. Manufacturers selecting champions will have more success looking for a distributor sales person who is new to distributor sales and a "B" performer who shows a lot of potential. B performers usually are not attached to a manufacturer's product line and are looking for ways to improve their performance and their expertise. RSMs informally select a salesperson to be their product specialist based on whom they work with most frequently and most comfortably.

The cooperation between the RSM and the distributor salesperson is critical to the success of the product line specialist concept. The RSM should enjoy the working relationship with a specific distributor salesperson, and the distributor salesperson should enjoy, admire, and respect the RSM. He or she should also admire the RSM's product knowledge and selling skills. The cooperation between the two parties may be formalized in a product champion or product line specialist program and eventually become part of the distributor contract. When using the champion concept, it is important to not ignore the owner, sales management or other influencers within the distributor's organization.

How can the RSM win a potential champion's respect? Most salespeople evaluate other salespeople on one simple criterion, "How good are they on a sales call?" Consequently, the first step in winning respect is demonstrating superior product and market knowledge, selling skills, and sales results. After a potential champion has observed the RSM conduct an effective and expert sales call, he or she will want to learn more about how the RSM operates in a sales environment.

What is in it for the champion? Distributor salespeople are looking for ways to improve. Their initial benefit is gaining knowledge and skills. They also gain a coach, mentor, and personal sales manager. Ultimately, they gain increased commissions and career enhancement.

Coaching the champion starts as soon as the RSM and champion have connected and the RSM has gained respect and credibility. Coaching starts with a conversation about the champion's possible role with the manufacturer's product line. Once the relationship is initiated, goals and expectations are established, and both parties are ready to begin more formal coaching.

Initially, RSMs must dedicate at least two days a month to coaching the product-line specialist or champion. After six months, the frequency may drop to one day a month with increased communications via e-mail and telephone. Coaching obviously requires a tremendous amount of work, so the number of product champions a specific RSM can develop is limited to two or three a year.

When should the RSM expect sales results from a champion or product-line specialist? Salespeople who are trying hard to succeed do not have smooth growth curves. Ambition and hard work yield jagged growth charts. Sale successes and failures are the norm before a more consistent methodology is developed. Erratic spikes indicate effort and call for continued coaching. The worst case is slow growth. Such a sales chart indicates the champion is playing it safe, not taking risks. Such an individual will probably not become a successful product champion or product-line specialist.

What are the functions of product-line champions? Their primary roles include the following:

- Being the primary contact person for communication and feedback with the RSM
- Maintaining all-around sales, technical, market, and process knowledge of the manufacturer's product line
- Assist other distributor sales team members in selling the manufacturers' products
- Assisting customer service and counter people as needed
- Taking on the mantle of leadership within the distributorship on all matters pertaining to the manufacturer's product line
- Receiving special recognition and incentives for successfully executing the product champion or specialist function
- Assisting the RMS in coordinating, setting up training sessions, mailings, promotions, and other key events

See Figure 11-3 for an example of one company's description of the functions of a product champion.

Reflection Point

Who are my product champions at the distributor level?
- How should I train them and recognize their efforts?
- Have I developed a written document of their primary functions?

Coaching Your Product-Line Specialist

RSMs will coach the product specialist or champion on a variety of skills necessary to excel in the sales, promotion, and inventory roles. The most important skill that the product champion must acquire is the ability to sell. The sales task can be broken down into observable behavioral components so that clear performance expectations

A Company Example—Product-Line Specialist, Primary Functions

A. Market Planning
1. Submit an annual market plan.
(The market plan includes competitive analysis, current sales, and financial performance.)

B. Market Development
1. Identify dealers by segment within the assigned area.
2. Identify qualified end users for direct sale.
3. Monitor and support sales efforts.

C. Inventory Management
1. In conjunction with purchasing and branch manager, set inventory levels for all equipment and parts.
2. Develop efficient delivery systems between branches to balance inventories and to the dealers within the assigned area.
3. In conjunction with purchasing, maintain balanced inventory levels at the branch locations.

D. Advertising and Promotions
1. Plan budgets and submit for approval, advertising, trade show participation, service and sales meetings, and promotion activities for products in conjunction with the regional sales manager.
2. Implement advertising and promotional plans as approved.
3. Monitor results of the plan.

E. Training
1. Schedule, promote, and coordinate dealer training seminars in conjunction with the regional sales manager.
2. Schedule, promote, and coordinate dealer sales training seminars in conjunction with the district sales manager.
3. Train all distributor branch personnel on policies with regard to warranty, product application, features, and benefits.

Figure 11-3. A company example: product-line specialist, primary functions (continued on the next page)

F. **Price Policies**
1. Determine price policies, volume discounts, and allowances.
2. Implement and enforce price policies.
3. Monitor and adjust as necessary.
4. Track profit contribution.

G. **Key Account Assignment**
1. Identify key accounts within the assigned area with high volume potential.
2. Develop special programs to meet key account needs.
3. Monitor and track sales performance versus potential.

H. **Performance Measurement**
1. Sales volume versus forecast.
2. Performance index improvement or gains in market share.
3. Gross profit percentage.
4. Gross profit (dollars) generated annually versus average monthly inventory.
5. GMROII (GP $ annual divided by inventory monthly).

Figure 11-3. A company example: product-line specialist, primary functions (continued)

can be set and behavior can be observed, analyzed, and modified through coaching.

The primary components of the sales job are product and market knowledge, selling skills, time and territory organization, account prioritization, and account strategy. Some of these sales job components are dictated by the distributorship. The areas where the manufacturer's RSM can most contribute are product, market and application knowledge, and selling skills.

Selling skills are a particularly difficult area to coach because it is difficult to break them down into component behaviors while allowing for differences of individual style. However, standards for selling skills must be established before coaching can begin. Most sales coaches and trainers agree that business to business selling skills can be organized around the four steps of the buying process—building *relationships* with the seller, clarifying *motivation* to buy, *evaluating*

Relationship	Judging the sales individual and the organization to be relevant, competent, trustworthy, receptive, and prepared. Importance to buying decision: 50%.
Motivation	Goals, improvements, or problems that are urgent, high priority, clear, fundable and justified. Importance to buying decision: 35%.
Evaluation	Gathering information for process, people, and criteria to make an evaluation. Importance to buying decision: 10%
Decision	Consensus and final concerns before commitment. Importance to buying decision: 5%.

Buyer's Stage	**Salesperson's Skills**
1. Relationship	▶ Preparation of self and materials ▶ Statement of call purpose and process
2. Motivation	▶ Questioning ▶ Listening ▶ Summary of key priorities
3. Evaluation	▶ Client-centered sales message ▶ Beneficial, involving, and visual presentation
4. Decision	▶ Build consensus ▶ Handle objections ▶ Gain commitment

Figure 11-4. The customer's buying process

relevant alternatives, and *deciding* on the best product or solution—as listed in Figure 11-4. The literature varies little on the four buyer stages just outlined. The literature varies more widely on how a salesperson should handle each of the four stages of the buying process.

Establishing clear expectations for selling behaviors at each step of the buying process is a critical start to the sales coaching. Distributor salespeople have unique challenges working through the buyer's process and execution of the selling skills. The following is a discussion of those challenges and of ideas manufacturers are using to assist distributor salespeople to be more effective.

Building Relationships

In the relationship stage of the buying process, distributor salespeople have a unique challenge because they make many more calls per day than most manufacturer salespeople. Consequently they have little time for customized preparation for sales calls. The result is sales calls that become routine. Interactions with existing customers are basically, "How are things going?" and "Do you need anything today?"

Most distributor sales calls are to existing customers. The relationship is already established, so the challenge for the salespeople is to introduce new ideas or benefits every time they call. Creating beneficial reasons for a sales call requires time, research, and creativity by the distributor salesperson. Many manufacturers are working with distributors to develop a variety of valid and beneficial reasons for sales calls to existing customers. Figure 11-5 contains an example of the reasons one company helped its distributors identify and use when calling on existing customers.

Note: This call is a distributor call on a dealer in a two-step channel

▶ 80-90% of your business comes from established customers. Your competitors, however, view your customers as potential new accounts. Therefore, you can assume that the competition will pursue your customers aggressively.

▶ Maintenance calls can be the most difficult call unless you have a clear objective. The maintenance call should reinforce the value of your relationship. Start by clearly stating the beneficial purpose of your call. Before you proceed, ask your customer if there are other issues they want to discuss. The following are examples of call objectives and opening statements.

Leads
I have a prequalified lead for you. I believe this customer will want to lease two new units.

Product Improvement
I have literature and price lists on the new X500. The X500 will open new markets for you in the construction sector. How do you currently fill the need for this type of product?

Figure 11-5. A company example: beneficial reasons to call on an existing customer (continued on next page)

Literature Update

There have been a few important literature changes in our product line brochure and our warranty policy. I'm here today to update your literature, toss the outdated literature, and make sure all your salespeople understand the changes.

Market Knowledge

Because of the poor water conditions in our area, a high percentage of users must precondition the water supply. I believe there is an opportunity for you to increase revenue on each sale by presenting a water filter. I want to discuss the possibility of training your salespeople on water problems and our filtration solutions.

Success Story

Some of our dealers started a rental program one year ago and are currently generating $100,000/month in revenue. I believe your company has a similar opportunity. How are you currently meeting the demand in lease sales situations?

Product Features

I want to talk to you about new control panel options that will give your customers the ability to match their existing electronics. We believe we can increase your sales though this unique offering.

Missed Opportunity

I've noticed that your company sells very few set-up and support services. I'm afraid your salespeople may be missing a very lucrative market segment.

Stock Levels

I would like to discuss our guaranteed inventory program today. In what situations are immediate product availability a key competitive advantage?

Sales Call Assistance

Occasionally we are called to assist a dealer on a particular or unusual application of our product or just to help close a difficult sale. Let's look at your upcoming calls to see if we can be of benefit to your sales team in similar situations.

Figure 11-5. A company example: beneficial reasons to call on an existing customer (continued on next page)

Upcoming Service Schools

The technicians that attend our service schools report increased productivity and fewer callbacks. We sponsor several of them in this area each year. I would like to discuss which of your service people you feel should attend our tech seminar.

Program Review

Borrowing money in today's market is getting more difficult. We've noticed a dramatic increase in new lease applications. During the same period, your lease activity has remained constant. I want to talk to your salespeople today about how a leasing program can increase their sales, commissions, and profits.

Promotion

We have a new promotion. This program can increase your sales and provide a real incentive for your salespeople.

Sales Training

I would like to discuss the productivity increases we've experienced from our sales training programs at a number of our dealers in this area.

Figure 11-5. A company example: beneficial reasons to call on an existing customer (continued)

Another skill distributor salespeople can improve is calling on new customers. Distributors rarely make new business development calls and are consequently not well practiced. Too often, distributors lead business development calls with one of the following questions, "Is there anything you can't get from your current suppliers?" or "How could I earn your business?" or "Could I get you a quote on that?" These approaches are fraught with problems. The price problem is obvious, and going head-to-head with the existing supplier is rarely successful. RSM coaching can help distributors develop a "foot in the door" strategy based on their best product or a new application.

Distributor salespeople too often work exclusively with buyers or purchasing managers who are driven to reduce price. Distributor salespeople need to build higher-level relationships in client organizations where increased quality or enhanced productivity benefits are more likely to get a fair hearing.

RSMs can participate in several types of sales calls to help the product champion strengthen the relationship with customers, including lead-by-example calls, shared calls, or coaching calls. In a lead-by-example call, the RSM demonstrates desired behavior; this is usually where coaching activity starts because observation is a good first learning step. This approach also increases credibility and trust and demonstrates that the RSM is willing to take a risk on behalf of the champion.

The shared call is often used with "A" accounts to optimize sales results because it uses the best qualities of both individuals. It is not an opportunity to coach; it is an opportunity to help. The coaching call is usually the last type of call executed. This call requires great trust and openness to feedback on the part of the champion. The champion conducts the call while the RSM observes. After the call the RSM gives positive and constructive feedback along with ideas for improvement. Being personally coached is one of the most valuable experiences salespeople can have as they develop.

Motivation

The second phase of the buying process is motivation, which for years has been referred to as "finding customer needs." But in an oversupplied economy with tough competitors, an unfilled customer need is rare. It is more productive to look for customer goals or priorities to find motivation to drive a buying cycle. Questioning, listening, and summarizing are the primary selling skills used to identify customer goals, desired improvements, priorities, or problems. Questioning is a weakness for most distributor salespeople because they have been taught to demonstrate and ask for the order. But that *old-school* method of selling is fading away—as are the distributors who use it.

A key transition for distributors is the acquisition of consultative selling skills.[1] Manufacturers are training distributor salespeople to ask better questions. The example questionnaire shown in Figure 11-6, lists questions for different sales call situations. Manufacturers are training distributor sales people to ask more questions and also to differentiate questioning strategies by market segment, stage of the sales cycle, or the products and services being discussed.

The second type of questioning skills is employed with existing customers. Developing questions for existing customers is difficult because so much more is known about them. The questions have to

Company #1: An Adapted List of Resource Questions for First Calls on Contractors

1. Could I ask you a few questions about your business?
2. How did you get started as a contractor?
3. How long have you been in the business?
4. How is your customer base mixed between commercial, industrial, and residential accounts?
5. Could we tour your facility while we talk?
6. What type of customers do you target?
7. What is your company best known for?
8. What is your geographic area of coverage?
9. How many service trucks do you have?
10. What is your greatest business challenge today?
11. How do you keep your service techs up to date?
12. What types of jobs give you the most trouble?
13. How do you try to balance the cost of inventory with the problems of being out of stock?
14. When you choose a new supplier, what do you look for?

Company #2: Questions Developed by Contractor Segments

Equipment Dealers

Business Name: _____

Address: _____

Telephone: _____

Contact Name:_____

1. What territory do you cover?
2. What market segments do you concentrate on?
3. What competitive advantage works best for your sales team?
4. How are they assigned: by account, geography, market, or other?

Service Dealers

Business Name: _____

Address: _____

Telephone: _____

Contact Name:_____

Figure 11-6. Company #1: An adapted list of resource questions for first calls on contractors (continued on next page)

1. What area do you service?
2. How many service people do you have? How many trucks?
3. What type of customers do you do the most work for?
4. What's your most effective way of getting new business?

Questions by Product or Service Function
1. What equipment, manufacturer, model size, and serial number of part do you need?
2. How soon do you need them?
3. Why did the equipment fail?
4. How long had that part been in service?
5. Do you have a record of how frequently this particular part is serviced, repaired, and replaced?
6. Are you going to need related parts?
7. Any other truck stock or future job parts we should add to this order?

Figure 11-6. Company #1: An adapted list of resource questions for first calls on contractors (continued)

be more specific and focused on change. Examples of questions used by distributors with existing customers are shown in Figure 11-7. Intelligent questioning is designed to identify customer motivation and priorities and is the first step in determining motivation.

Standard Opening Questions
1. General greeting:
   ▶ "How is it going?"
   ▶ "How are you doing?"
   ▶ "It looks like business is picking up a bit. What type of jobs have picked up the most?"
2. The beneficial reason for the call today:
   ▶ "We have several new processes and products to help you build your business servicing indoor air quality (IAQ) problems. I'd like to discuss them with you and see if you think they could help you better serve some of your key accounts."
3. Getting at their issues for today's meeting:
   ▶ "Before we discuss the new IAQ programs, has anything changed that you want to cover today?"

Figure 11-7. Existing customer questionnaire (continued on next page)

4. Follow-up from your last call or ongoing business issues:
   ▶ "Last time we met you asked about our new line. I have two samples with me today."

Account Customized Mid-Interview Questions

5. Discussion of your beneficial reason for the meeting:
   ▶ "Our new IAQ programs and products assist you in serving your market."
6. Specific account benefit discussion:
   ▶ "I've been studying your parts orders, quantities, and inventory. I think we can save money by putting you on a weekly EDI ordering system and schedule to reduce your order and inventory costs."
7. Ask about performance:
   ▶ "Our goal is to give you outstanding service, support, training, and quality products."
   ▶ "How do we rate compared to your other best suppliers?"
   ▶ "Anything we've done badly?"
   ▶ "What could we improve on?"
8. Ask about change:
   ▶ "Is your business mix changing?"
   ▶ "What products are selling best right now? Why?"
   ▶ "Are you focusing on any new accounts or types of business?"
   ▶ "Have you made any recent personnel changes?"
9. Ask about current information, support, training, and product needs:
   ▶ "Do you have any techs who need training?"
   ▶ "What products do we need to make sure get ordered today? Any of them need special handling or unusually quick delivery?"
   ▶ "Do you have the current literature?"
   ▶ "Is there anything we need to discuss that we haven't covered yet?"
   ▶ "Is there anyone else I should talk to while I'm here?"

Standard Closing Questions

10. Summary of the call and next action:
    ▶ "I'll send you the IAQ video tomorrow and call you at the end of the week with three dates for an IAQ training session. I'll also expedite your order. Is that everything?"

Figure 11-7. Existing customer questionnaire (continued on next page)

> 11. Setting your next meeting:
>   ▶ "I'll be back two weeks from Thursday—that's the 27th at 9:00 am—to follow up on the IAQ service school and to make sure you've got the equipment you need to start making IAQ calls. Will that time work for you?"

Figure 11-7. Existing customer questionnaire (continued)
Note: Adapted from distribution training materials

After asking relevant questions to uncover buying motives, salespeople must listen to the customer's answers. Listening is an underdeveloped selling skill for many distributor salespeople because their history of making many short calls left little time for real listening. Distributor salespeople should keep four rules about listening in mind.

1. At least 50 percent of any sales call should be spent listening to the customer.
2. Listen actively and take notes.
3. Listen selectively and reinforce key customer motivations.
4. Summarize the customer's top priorities and ask for confirmation of his or her purchasing priorities.

Consider this example of a summary of customer motivation:

Let me summarize. You want an ice machine that will fit in this 26 inch space in the kitchen, be more reliable than your previous ice machine, and produce at least 1,000 pounds of ice a day, even in the summertime. Are those your top priorities for your new machine?

If you have listened well and asked the right questions, customers will validate your summary or correct it. In either case, the customer feels understood, and that feeling is critical to sales success. It is important to note that 80 to 85 percent of the buying process and product preference is complete at this point.

Evaluation

The third stage of the buying process is the "evaluation" of alternative solutions. At this stage, the customer is looking at alternatives, gathering final information, and developing clear product preferences. Coaching sales people to make effective and focused sales presentations requires an approach that can be successfully passed through down-stream channel members and to end users. Distributor sales presentations are short and therefore need to "cut to the chase" quickly. Presentations should consist of only a few key points to mirror the summary of customer key motivations.

Remember the *BIV* process when presenting your sales points. Start with the product's *Benefit,* then *Involve* the customer in the presentation, and finally make the sales point *Visible.* The customer must see a difference to believe it.

As an example, Penda Corporation sells its truck bed liner through warehouse distributors, who resell it to retailers, who sell it to truck owners. The benefit of its premium bed liner, the Skid Resistor™, is that the liner's texture prevents a load from sliding around in the back of a truck. This intangible sales point is difficult for distributors or retailers to articulate to truck owners. To enable distributors to follow the BIV model, Penda put two small sections of bed liners, theirs and a competitors, on a 30-degree angled board. A paint can sits on top of the display. The customer is asked to place the paint can on both bed liners. The paint can slides off the competitive bed liner but sticks to the Penda Skid Resistor bed liner. This simple and visible proof involves the customer and makes the benefit clear. Any time a manufacturer can create such an effective point-of-sale aid, it will build belief *within* the channel and sales *through* the channel.

Another way manufacturers can help improve distributor presentations is in the positioning of price. Instead of waiting for price pressure, manufacturers are encouraging distributors to take the offensive and position price by proving value to the customer.

Harley-Davidson salespeople provide a good example of positioning price in a sales presentation. Their claim is simple, straightforward, and powerful. They tell customers that you can buy another brand of motorcycle for $10,000, drive it for five years, and then sell it for $5,000. The annual cost of ownership of that motorcycle is $1,000 per year. Or, you can buy a Harley Davidson for $15,000 and sell it in five years for $15,000. The annual cost of ownership is zero. The obvious question to the customer is, "Which is the better value: $1,000 per year or zero?"

To maintain price integrity, manufacturers must provide distributors a price-positioning story that is persuasive and easy to tell.

Manufacturers who wish to get their story told must also make it visible, fun, beneficial, and involving.

Decision

The last stage of the buying process involves making the final purchase decision and committing to a course of action. The buyer normally feels some level of anxiety and expresses it as concerns or objections. Experienced salespeople handle objections by accepting, listening, probing, and then providing relevant information to satisfy the customer's concern. Less experienced salespeople see objections as stumbling blocks and try to immediately overcome them with counter arguments.

The RSM can coach the product-line champions by first modeling the correct behavior and then teaching them how to do it. Once objections are overcome and consensus is achieved, all that is left is asking for the order. Most distributor salespeople are comfortable asking for the order, so this is usually not a significant stumbling block or coaching opportunity.

Once all the aspects of buying and selling have been discussed in detail, the RSM should create a list of selling skill expectations. See Figure 11-8 for an example of a detailed list of selling skills expectations in a sales call evaluation form. When the RSM and product-line champion review sales calls, they will have a common language and a common set of expectations to guide their discussion. Establishing clear expectations is a prerequisite to effective coaching. After that, the RSM coach observes sales calls, discusses selling skills that could be improved, and then works with the champion or specialist to make the desired changes.

Beyond selling skills, the RSM will teach the product-line specialist about inventory management, developing promotions, advertising, and lead generation programs, and explain the use of cooperative advertising dollars. The RSM must also educate the specialist on policies, warranty, returns, and technical support procedures. The champion will be the point person on updating literature and keeping the information flow between the manufacturer and all distributor personnel. It is important to remember that the RSM is creating an inspirational leader at the distributorship. The enthusiasm, respect, and

Actions	Oops	So So	Good	Great	Comments

Relationship
1. Preparation of self and
    materials
2. Initial impression; clearly
    stated objective
	1
	
	1
		2
		
		2
			3
			
			3
				4
				
				4	

Motivation
3. Questioning for goals,
    needs, priorities, decision
    maker, criteria, and process
4. Listening for central ideas,
    listen over 50% of the time
5. Summary of top three
    motivators
	1
	
	1
	
	1
		2
		
		2
		
		2
			3
			
			3
			
			3
				4
				
				4
				
				4	

Evaluation
6. Client-focused information
    only
7. Benefit, involve, visible
    (BIV)
	1
	
	1
		2
		
		2
			3
			
			3
				4
				
				4	

Decision
8. Reach consensus
9. Handled objections and
    concerns
10. Gained commitment to a
    specific action
	1
	
	1
	
	1
		2
		
		2
		
		2
			3
			
			3
			
			3
				4
				
				4
				
				4	

Figure 11-8. Sales call evaluation form

credibility the champion achieves will be the single most important element of implementation of the manufacturer's sales plan.

Reflection Point

> **How well do I coach my product champions?**
> ▶ Have I developed clear expectations for selling skills?
> ▶ Has my company provided sales tools that BIV our product advantages?

Distributor Sales Training

The first step in sales training is convincing distribution personnel that sales training is a good investment of their time and energy. It's a tough sell. The distributor owner needs to be convinced that the training will lead to greater margin, profit, and efficiencies. The sales manager needs to know that the training will improve sales results, selling skills, and customer and employee retention. The sales team needs to know the training will enhance their compensation, be fun, and make their job easier. This is a multilevel complex sale, and the product is intangible.

If the RSM can sell training, it speaks well of his or her selling skills and the distributor's willingness to work with its manufacturing partners. The following list includes some of the best RSM ideas to make the concept of sales training more acceptable and saleable to distributors.

1. Base training goals on the distributor's business goals. The RSM should not limit training to the features and benefits of their manufacturers' products.
2. Make training relevant to the most difficult sales situations, such as handling price objections, selling uniqueness, or differential advantage.
3. Sell a training schedule for the year; don't sell training programs one event at a time. When selling an annual training schedule, be flexible to meet distributor time requirements and go for short but frequent training sessions instead of a few long sessions.
4. Build incentives into the training so distributors know training results will be tracked and incentives can be achieved.
5. Build on small successes. Very few training programs are fully attended in the first year they are offerred. It usually takes several years before a training program grows in acceptance and popularity. One of the best ways to build training program credibility is through testimony from people who have attended and achieved success.
6. Use a sales trainer who has credibility with the distributor salespeople.

What types of training sessions are most valuable and motivational for distributor salespeople? Short, informative, and frequent sessions work best. Distributor salespeople are busy and have limited time available for training. Each session should focus on just one or two items.

Make training fun. Get the salespeople involved; structure positive exercises, group activities, and refreshments to build enjoyment and learning. Make training relevant to their daily client interactions. Train everyone who has customer contact—including counter and inside salespeople. Figure 11-9 provides an example of the type of information counter and inside salespeople should acquire during product training.

Questions to Ask Counter and Inside Salespeople after Training

Product Analysis

1. *Name* of product line _____
   What is it? _____
   What is its *function*? _____
   Scope of the line _____
   Where does it fit in the system? _____
   How do you *size it*? _____

2. Three questions to understand the *customer's needs*:

   _____
   _____
   _____

3. Three key sales points in *feature and benefit* format (a feature is physical, and a benefit is what it does for the customer)

   _____
   _____
   _____

4. How will you *involve* the customer with the product?

   _____
   _____

5. How will you make the product *visible* to the customer?

   _____
   _____

6. Logical *add-on* sale items

   _____
   _____

7. Top competitors

Names	Key sales points
_____	_____
_____	_____
_____	_____

Figure 11-9. Counter and inside sales product training (continued on next page)

Sell Sheets

Product name _____

Questions

_____

_____

Key selling points

_____

_____

_____

_____

BIV sales aids

_____

_____

Objections and answers

_____   _____

                                   _____

                                   _____

_____   _____

Add-ons

_____

_____

Figure 11-9. Counter and inside sales product training (continued)

Keep training simple. Keep the agenda short and focused. If training wanders off task, the central point is compromised. Make training positive and energetic. Train on specific market segments or customer types. Recognize individuals for their success in the market place since the last session. Finally, before you put together any training session, always ask yourself, "What behavior do I want to see changed as a result of this training?" If you can answer that question clearly, you have an excellent chance of developing an effective training program.

Training Evaluation

Regional sales managers need to evaluate their training sessions. The following points may aid evaluation efforts:

- ▶ Did I have a written purpose and agenda for the meeting?
- ▶ Was it fun?
- ▶ Was it short and information packed?

▶ Did I combine sales information and selling skills in role-playing?
▶ Was it relevant to their problems?
▶ Was there plenty of participation?
▶ Was the required behavior change clear and accomplished?

Manufacturers are always seeking ways to improve training sessions. Figure 11-10 provides a template for an evaluation form that provides action-oriented feedback, solicits ideas for future training, and identifies potential training recommendations. Perhaps the most relevant feedback from training is whether more or fewer people attend the next training session offered.

Not all RSMs make good trainers. As a result, many manufacturers have begun outsourcing training to professionals so that distributors can experience high quality and effective training sessions.

Training incentives can be structured to encourage attendees to use the training. For example, some manufacturers allow training expenses to qualify as a co-op expenditure; that is, the training expense is shared 50 percent by the manufacturer and 50 percent by the distributor. Further incentives for distributor training can be based on post-training sales performance. For example, if a distributor's sales results go up 10 percent in the quarter following training, then 10 percent of the distributor's training expenses will be reimbursed. The idea of building incentives into post-workshop sales performance assures measurement, motivation, and reward.

As a final test for your training programs, ask your distributors to name the top three selling points of your product line. Compare their answers to your original message. Their diverse responses indicate how clearly your message is getting to the market. Training needs to be clear, simple, and repeated frequently.

Dealer Training

Lack of consistency of message through a channel of distribution is a common problem. Training at the distributor level may not be the entire solution. Many companies have started dealer training, and a few have even initiated end-user training. Many manufacturing companies have been "burned" by ignoring the levels below the distributor and not doing dealer or end-user training.

Actions	Oops	So So	Good	Great	Ideas for Improvement
1. Clear written objective and agenda	1	2	3	4	
2. Fun	1	2	3	4	
3. Short	1	2	3	4	
4. Connected product features to customer benefits	1	2	3	4	
5. Relevant to their sales situation	1	2	3	4	
6. Participation, participation	1	2	3	4	
7. Role-played and tested desired behavior change	1	2	3	4	

Note: To check if the training was retained, test and role play again in three months.

Program Name: _____   Date:_____

   1. What was the most useful part of the workshop for you?

   _____

   2. What parts were of little or no value to you?

   _____

   3. What will you do differently based on this training?

   _____

   4. What subjects would you like to see covered in future training sessions?

   _____

   5. Would you recommend the workshop to others? Why?

   _____
   _____

                                     Name_____
                                               (optional)

Figure 11-10. Evaluate your own sales training sessions

Joseph Conlin, writing in *Sales and Marketing Management,* summarizes this concept. He states, "While you boast of new distribution channels, your dealer may be abandoning your company for the competition. Want to win their loyalty back? Run meetings just for them." Joseph further notes that a company must "run meetings that emphasize education and recognition."[2] He goes on further to note that these meetings also teach market segmentation. The training message should be delivered to the entire channel to assure the message gets through to the most important level, the end-user decision maker.

Reflection Point	**How often do we train distributor sales and technical people?** ▶ Do they attend eagerly? ▶ How do we measure training effectiveness?

Using Promotions and Advertising

One method used by manufacturers to assist distributors in promoting their products is the cooperative advertising fund (co-op fund). Cooperative advertising is a shared advertising expense budget. Figure 11-11 is an example of a typical co-op advertising program for one particular manufacturer.

The manufacturer will match the distributor's budget up to a defined amount. The amount is usually set between one or two percent of total sales for the previous year. From the manufacturer's perspective, the co-op fund doubles the distributor's promotion budget and gives them some control over how the money is invested. Co-op dollars must be invested in valid or approved promotions. Normally, co-op money must be used within the prescribed budget year and not rolled forward into future years. Figure 11-12 shows how the co-op or promotion reserve fund investments are recorded by month and by type of activity.

Manufacturers often wonder whether their distributors are investing co-op funds wisely. To help distributors be more effective, manufacturers may do one of two things. First, they may educate the distributors on how to make better use of advertising investment, or provide them a menu of high-quality ads and promotions so distributors can pick the ones that best fit their local market area. Both of these approaches have proved successful.

Procedure #	**Date Issued:** **Date Effective:** **Latest Revision:**
Promotion Reserve **Fund Program**	

Purpose: To encourage and assist the distributor in promotion

Scope: This procedure defines the Promotion Reserve Fund program and the process to accrue and claim cooperative assistance. The Promotion Reserve Fund is available to all distributors who achieve $100,000 or more volume in sales/purchases in a calendar year.

References:
6. Promotion Planning Calendar
7. Promotion Claim Form
8. Sample Report Promotion Reserve Statement

Instructions:
2.1 Promotion Reserve Fund Program
    2.1.1 Accrues 1.5% of net equipment purchases for promotional use during the following calendar year.
    2.1.2 With the assistance of the district sales manager, the distributor submits an annual promotion plan and budget.
    2.1.3 The distributor secures approval from the advertising coordinator for each promotional activity, in advance.
    2.1.4 The Promotion Reserve Fund is a cooperative fund.
        2.1.4.1 Reimburses the distributor 50% of the approved promotional expenses during the calendar year.
        2.1.4.2 Cumulative claims cannot exceed the fund accrual.
        2.1.4.3 In the event the promotion involves multiple suppliers, reimburses the distributor 50% of proportionate expense.
    2.1.5 The distributor submits claims with appropriate documentation of expenses within thirty (30) days of promotion completion.
        2.1.5.1 Claims for the fourth (calendar) quarter are due by January 31.

Figure 11-11. Cooperative plan (continued on next page)

2.1.5.2 Claims received after January 31 for promotion occurring in the preceding year will be rejected.
2.1.6 The fund is available for use during the calendar year.
    2.1.6.1 The distributor forfeits any unused portion after January for the preceding calendar year.
    2.1.6.2 The distributor cannot draw on the following calendar year accrual.
2.2 Promo Reserve Statement
  2.2.1 The distributor will receive a Promotion Reserve Statement, indicating claim activity and balance in current year's fund, on a quarterly basis.
2.3 Approved Expenditures
  2.3.1 Approved Yellow Page advertising.
  2.3.2 Mailings to dealers or other types of customers within the distributor's area of primary selling responsibility as defined in the distributor agreement.
  2.2.3 Literature.
  2.2.4 Sale promotion items.
  2.2.5 Trade show and exhibitions.
  2.2.6 Special promotions for dealers or dealer sales representatives.
  2.2.7 Factory visits by customers or distributor personnel.
  2.2.8 Expenditures for sales and/or service meetings.
  2.2.9 Local newspaper, trade magazines, radio, or TV advertising.
Other advertising and promotion activities with preapproval of the advertising coordinator.

Figure 11-11. Cooperative plan (continued)

The first problem encountered when assisting distributors' promotional efforts is their relative lack of customer targeting. Distributors target all their customers with the same promotion. Such promotions violate fundamental rules in advertising: know precisely to whom you are talking and what message will resonate with each target group. Figure 11-13 shows four stages of customer relationships, including *suspects, prospects, customers,* and *advocates.* Each should receive different communications. In the case of an *advocate,* you are trying to increase loyalty and volume purchases. With a *prospect,* you are looking for the first order.

Distributor: _____   District Manager: _____

City: _____   State: _____

Contact: _____

Promotion Reserve Allocation: $_____   Purchases: $_____

Matching Distributor Portion: $_____

Total to be Budgeted: $_____

Promotional Activity	Jan	Feb	Mar	Apr	May	Jun	Jul	Aug	Sep	Oct	Nov	Dec	Tot
Yellow Pages													
Literature													
Trade Shows													
Advertising													
Giveaways													
Direct Mail													
Open House/Awards													
Sales Seminars													
Sales Training													
Contests/Incentives													
Tickets/Tournaments													
Miscellaneous													
TOTAL													

Figure 11-12. Promotion reserve

Customer Stage	Strategy	Message
Advocate	Reinforce	Frequent buyer incentive, floor plan consignment, joint promotions, stocking programs
Customer	Support	Accumulative incentives, leads, gifts, and premiums
Prospect	Qualify	Trial programs, testimonial, guarantees, and qualifying questions
Suspect	Initiate contact	Mailing offer with response card, referrals, events, telephone, and cold calls, samples, tours

Figure 11-13. The message for different stages of customer development

As shown in Figure 11-14, a particular manufacturer identified contractor market segments with the above loyalty segments, resulting in a 16-cell grid. Identifying the accounts in each cell (e.g., residential contractors who are advocates) allows a more careful targeting of advertising messages.

	Residential	Commercial	Industrial	Mechanical
Advocate				
Customer				
Prospect				
Suspect				

Figure 11-14. Customer segmentation chart

The next critical decisions are media, frequency, and timing. Where the message appears, how often, and when is as or more important than the message itself. Finally, decisions on wording and layout can be completed. Most distributors develop promotions backwards. They start by wording a message, designing layout and body copy, and then backing up to the media decision; they rarely even get to the target audience or action desired.

Here are a few take-away thoughts from promotions and advertising. It is better to have an average message that is a direct hit on your target market than to have a terrific promotion that is shown to the wrong people. Second, exposure frequency is more persuasive than one high-impact exposure. If you can't afford to make three exposures, don't invest in the first one. Third, selecting a tight target and a clear objective are the first steps in creating promotions.

Some manufacturers contract for the creation of professional promotional materials for their distributors. The distributors select the promotions that best fit their local market situation. This approach has been a significant aid to distributors because they are more competent at choosing than creating promotions.

Customer-customized promotions have become more common. Instead of running a standard "dinner-for-two" promotion for all customers, distributor salespeople are customizing promotions for individual customers. The customer may prefer a team outing to a ball game, a golf tournament, or a donation to a favorite charity. The salesperson who has key account responsibility decides how the promotional fund money should be spent. These customized promotions have been very successful because they can be fully adapted to customer organizations, values, and personalities. It also empowers the salespeople to know they control a substantial amount of the promotional budget.

> **Reflection Point**
>
> **How are we helping our distributors improve their promotion and advertising?**
> ▶ How are we measuring our co-op fund investment?
> ▶ How are we measuring our distributor's advertising effectiveness?

Acting as a Business Consultant

For at least the past 20 years, salespeople have been told to "be a consultant" to their clients. However, very few organizations bother to train the salespeople to consult. A consultant needs a well-defined set of skills and attitudes to be effective.

First, the attitude must be to help the client organization achieve its goals, not simply to sell them the manufacturer's products. Second, a consultant must be financially astute and a skilled business planner and strategist. Finally, a consultant must have relevant experience in the type of business and industry in which they consult. Most manufacturing companies don't really want their salespeople to act as true consultants because it would not always be in their own best interest; consequently, they don't train them in the skills required. In fact, job descriptions usually hold salespeople responsible primarily for sales volume—not consulting excellence.

So, what kind of business consultant should RSMs be to the distributors they serve? They should provide industry expertise and expert ideas related to product-line decisions and bottom-line results. This is a more practical and accurate description of what manufacturers mean when they say "act like a consultant" to our distributors. Although it is not true consulting, it is a valuable service that will strengthen the manufacturer/distributor relationship and possibly win greater mind share with the distributor than your product-line sales would justify.

Key Points

- ▶ Manufacturers' RSMs must approach the distributor channel like a national account—a multilevel, complex sale with a strategic annual account plan.
- ▶ RSMs need to develop champions or product-line specialists within each distributor so they will have a key contact point and inspirational leader within each of their distributors.
- ▶ A RSM's job requires multiple areas of expertise: selling, coaching, developing product-line champions, training, sales assistance, advertising and promotions, inventory management, and consultant to the distributor owner.
- ▶ Anything the manufacturer can do to make its product advantage beneficial, involving, and *visible* (BIV) will enhance point-of-sale effort and success for the distributor.

Notes

1. Two good books on the topic of consultative selling are Neil Rackham, *Spin Selling* (McGraw-Hill, 1988), and Thomas Freese, *The Secrets of Question-Based Selling* (Sourcebooks Trade, 2002).
2. Joseph Conlin, "The Art of the Dealer Meeting," *Sales & Marketing Management*, February 1997, pp. 77-81.

Chapter 12

MONITORING PERFORMANCE AND ADJUSTING PLANS

The final step in channel design is the ongoing process of monitoring performance and taking corrective actions. This is Stage VII, as shown in Figure 12-1. In this chapter, the primary methods for monitoring distributor performance and making appropriate adjustments are discussed.

Performance Monitoring

There are three methods for monitoring distributor performance: sales results, sales activities, and execution of planned changes. Each of these has advantages and disadvantages, and typically some combination of all three works the best.

Monitoring Sales Results

Monitoring distributor performance is most frequently and accurately done by monitoring sales results, which usually appear as purchases and drop-shipment orders. The problem with using sales results for monitoring distribution performance is the lag time between effort and result. Sales results occur long after sales effort

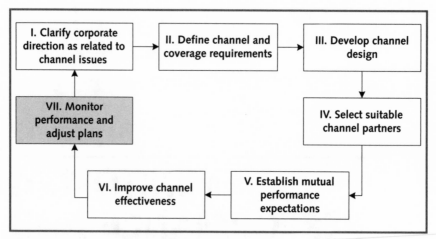

Figure 12-1. Stage VII of channel redesign

has taken place. Consequently, such analysis occurs too late to lead to timely corrective actions. Manufacturers monitor comparative distributor's penetration index to compare sales results with other distributors and channel members.

Manufacturers also monitor other quantifiable distributor performance indicators, such as inventory levels, the number of request for quotations (RFQs), the number of daily customer service calls, warranty registrations, the number of training sessions that the distributor sponsors, cooperative advertising expenses, and the number of sales calls made. These results can be measured weekly, monthly, and quarterly and are good general overall indicators of the distributor's sale activity level.[1]

Monitoring Activities

The second way to monitor distributors is to make the RSMs responsible for monitoring the quality and quantity of distribution activities in the marketplace. Activities, actions, or events are more subjective than sales results and often hard to quantify. The great advantage of monitoring activities is speed and adjustability.

Some potential activities to monitor are the quality of personnel dedicated as product-line champions, the quality of sales calls, technical and support personnel, number of requests for RSM sales assistance, the speed with which the distributor returns your phone calls, the ease with which the distributor can schedule training sessions, frequency of training sessions, and the number of attendees. The RSMs are also close to the co-op promotion program and can more effectively judge the effort and emphasis the distributor puts on using co-op dollars.

The RSM can observe and judge the quality and quantity of sales calls featuring their manufacturer's products. This happens by making sales calls with distributor's salespeople and observing the type of calls being made, the type of accounts being called on, the level or title of the client contact person, the receptivity and relationship with the customer, and the impact of the sales call.

Perhaps the most significant monitoring event is riding along on sales calls with the distributor sales champion. The quality of those calls is a critical variable in a manufacturer's goal achievement. The RSMs can also talk with counter, customer service, and inbound and outbound telemarketing personnel and determine their comfort level in recommending the manufacturer's product line.

Distributors sell the products they are most comfortable and confident in recommending. Monitoring activities at the distributorship provides a "feeling" for what will happen in the future. The RSMs can act as an early warning system by determining if a distributor is enthusiastic about your product line and is headed for growth, status quo, or decline.

Monitoring Change

The third and final way to monitor distributors is to determine whether they are making the significant changes called for in the business plan. Change items may be events such as adding a salesperson, adding a customer service person, adding a new geographic region, attending training sessions, increasing inventory in a specific product line, or introducing new promotional programs such as onsite or consignment inventory. Operational changes called for by the distributor's plan are assigned to an individual with a due date. It is a fairly simple matter for the RSM to monitor these dates and the quality of their execution.

The RSM has to exercise skill and judgment in monitoring activities and changes. None of these items is individually significant but put together they paint a reasonably clear picture of the distributor's intent, motivation, and dedication to the manufacturer's product line. A good and experienced RSM can accurately predict sales results based on the impression formed from all of the indicators available.

Monitoring allows manufacturers to make adjustments to existing business plans. If the adjustments are based solely on sales results, they will be made too late and will be ineffective in altering near-term outcomes. If the RSM's overall impression is formed early enough, adjustment may be timely enough and therefore have a better chance for success.

Reflection Point

What metrics do we use to evaluate distributor performance?
- ▶ What results do we monitor?
- ▶ How do we monitor distributor sales activities and business changes?
- ▶ How effective are we at initiating corrective actions?

Product-Line Performance Review

Another form of monitoring distributor performance, which uses all the elements discussed to this point, is called the product-line performance review. A product-line performance review is usually conducted once a year, roughly six months after mutual business planning has been completed. A formal product-line performance review uses an agreed-upon format and two-way communication. The distributor evaluates the performance of the manufacturer, and the manufacturer evaluates the performance of the distributor. The evaluation information is shared and should lead both parties to corrective action. The items on the next pages provide a comprehensive, formal, multipage product-line performance review format.

The first section is a review of results: sales by market, by product, and by branch. The second section computes earns and turns, and return on investment. Product-line sales are reported in detail by market segments and key accounts. The middle and largest section of the product-line performance review has several subsections, such as product, distribution, sales effort, promotions, warranty and returns, service and training.

Date: _____

Distributor: _____

Purchase History

	Product X	Product Y	Parts	Returns	Total
Current	$_____	$_____	$_____	($____)	$_____
One year ago	$_____	$_____	$_____	($____)	$_____
% change	$_____	$_____	$_____	($____)	$_____

Performance History

Performance Index	Product X	Product Y
Current	_____%	_____%
One year ago	_____%	_____%
National average	_____%	_____%

Cooperative Promotion Fund

	Allocation	Claimed	Percent
Recent calendar year	$_____	$_____	_____%
Previous calendar year	$_____	$_____	_____%

Sales Information

Total sales volume	$_____
Total number of employees	_____
Number outside sales	_____
Number inside sales	_____

Key Personnel

Name	Title	Responsibility
	President/Owner	
	Accounting	
	Purchasing/Inventory control	
	Sales manager	
	Product-line champion	

Primary Product Lines

Sales by Customer Segment

Number of Dealers	Type	Dollars	% of Total
	Service dealers	$_____	_____ %
	Independent contractors	$_____	_____ %
	Equipment dealers	$_____	_____ %
	Fabricators	$_____	_____ %
	Rental companies	$_____	_____ %
	Chains	$_____	_____ %
	Institutions	$_____	_____ %
	Government	$_____	_____ %

Product-Line Profitability

	Current Year
Gross sales equipment	$_____
Gross sales parts	$_____
Total Sales	$_____
Cost of sales equipment	$_____
Cost of sales parts	$_____
Total Cost of Sales	$_____
Average monthly inventory equipment	$_____
Average monthly inventory parts	$_____
Average Monthly Inventory Total	$_____
Earns and turns (total)	$_____
GMROII (Total)	$_____

Product

Goods or services produced to meet a customer's need (function).

Manufacturer Strategy: Design and produce goods that appeal to a broad customer base and are compatible with the current channels of distribution.

Key Measurement				
4	3	2	1	Products meet the users' need
4	3	2	1	Breadth of product line
4	3	2	1	Quality of products

Distributor Comments:

_____

_____

_____

Distributor Strategy: Offer products and other compatible products that reach the same target, end user, through common dealer channels.

Key Measurement				
4	3	2	1	Products are compatible but not competitive
4	3	2	1	Products are sold exclusively through dealers
4	3	2	1	Offers the complete line

Manufacturer Comments:

_____

_____

_____

Distribution

Activities associated with the movement of product from manufacturer to end user				

Manufacturer Strategy: To deliver undamaged product to the end user, on demand, in all major markets, and within 24 hours.

Key Measurement				
4	3	2	1	Fills 95% of all distributor orders from inventory and ships within 48 hours
4	3	2	1	Maintains a network of qualified service representatives to deliver, install, and start equipment on a national basis
4	3	2	1	Provide expedient service without freight damage

Distributor Comments:

_____

_____

_____

Distributor Strategy: To deliver undamaged product to the end user on demand, in the major markets, and within 24 hours anywhere within the assigned area.

Key Measurement				
4	3	2	1	Maintains balanced inventory
4	3	2	1	Fills 90% of all dealer orders from inventory
4	3	2	1	Tracks order fill rate
4	3	2	1	Maintains a network of service representatives to deliver, install, and start equipment

Manufacturer Comments:

_____

_____

_____

Sales Force

Representatives of a company whose goals is to reach, through personal contact, the distribution channels or end users and persuade them to buy.

Manufacturer Strategy: Organizes its sales force to support the distributor with sales training, product training, market planning and sales.

Key Measurement				
4	3	2	1	Provides sales and product training for each distributor salesperson
4	3	2	1	Provides sales and product training for each dealer salesperson
4	3	2	1	Provides market planning assistance
4	3	2	1	Assists on joint sales calls
4	3	2	1	Develops a product-line sales specialist

Distributor Comments:

_____

_____

_____

Distributor Strategy: Organizes its sales force for optimal geographic and dealer segment coverage to reach all targeted dealers.

Key Measurement				
4	3	2	1	Organizes its sales force to cover all of the assigned area
4	3	2	1	Has a defined strategy to seek new prospects
4	3	2	1	Provides effective sales representation as a product-line sales specialist
4	3	2	1	Sales force assignment by dealer segment
4	3	2	1	Sales representatives are knowledgable on product and services

Manufacturer Comments:

_____

_____

_____

Promotion

Advertising, merchandising, sales promotions, publicity, and other activities that enhance brand awareness and stimulate purchasing.				

Manufacturer Strategy: Promotes on a national level. General focus is to create end-user demand for the product.

Key Measurement				
4	3	2	1	Advertises effectively through national trade journals directed at various end users and dealer segments
4	3	2	1	Participates in national trade shows and generates quality leads
4	3	2	1	Provides promotion reserve funds to support promotional activities on a local level
4	3	2	1	Provides professional advertising and promotional materials

Distributor Comments:

_____

_____

_____

Distributor Strategy: Promotes on a local level. General focus is to strengthen and expand dealer loyalty for manufacturer.

Key Measurement				
4	3	2	1	Plans a balanced budget for promotional activities annually
4	3	2	1	Provides quality and frequent dealer sales training seminars
4	3	2	1	Advertises in local trade journals and publications to generate leads
4	3	2	1	Participates in local trade and dealer shows to generate leads
4	3	2	1	Sponsors effective promotions
4	3	2	1	Distributes and maintains current product literature

Manufacturer Comments:

_____

_____

_____

Warranty

A guarantee of quality and/or performance of a product or service by the manufacturer to the end user.				

Manufacturer Strategy: To minimize the inconvenience and cost in the event of a failure during the warranty period through efficient handling of warranty claims.

Key Measurement				
4	3	2	1	Offers the strongest warranty in the industry
4	3	2	1	Freight allowance policy on warranty returns
4	3	2	1	Resolves warranty returns and issues credit within 10 days

Distributor Comments:

_____

_____

_____

Distributor Strategy: Minimizes the inconvenience of a failure during the warranty period through efficient handling of warranty claims.

Key Measurement				
4	3	2	1	Registers warranties upon shipment
4	3	2	1	Issues credit promptly and without additional freight or handling charges

Manufacturer Comments:

_____

_____

_____

Service

Support functions that fulfill customer needs that are not necessarily tied to the sale of a product or another service.				

Manufacturer Strategy: Satisfy the customer's need for qualified technical support, including installation, operation, maintenance, and repair.

Key Measurement				
4	3	2	1	Conducts high-quality factory service training
4	3	2	1	Field service training is frequent and high quality
4	3	2	1	Publishes clear, easy to understand, technical manuals
4	3	2	1	Provides fast, friendly technical assistance

Distributor Comments:

_____

_____

_____

Distributor Strategy: Satisfy the customer's need for qualified technical support, including installation, operation, maintenance, and repair.

Key Measurement				
4	3	2	1	Promotes, schedules, and coordinates field service seminars
4	3	2	1	Promotes attendance at the factory service seminar by service representatives
4	3	2	1	Maintains and disseminates service bulletins, manuals, and technical materials to local service companies
4	3	2	1	Maintains a network of qualified service representatives

Manufacturer Comments:

_____

_____

_____

Each party reviews the other's performance and provides a rating and comments. The final section of the performance review is the identification of areas of concern and potential improvement, a plan for improvement with the actions, timing, and assignment of responsibility.

Both parties sign off on the review, and then the manufacturer takes appropriate action on behalf of the distributor, and the distributor takes appropriate action on behalf of the manufacturer. The product-line performance review and the mutual planning process described in Chapter 10 provides manufacturers and distributors with two formal occasions for business analysis and corrective adjustments. Closeness and collaboration almost guarantees successful implementation and increases the commitment to the relationship.

Distributor Councils

There are less direct ways to obtain distributor feedback and increase communication. The most common methods are distributor councils and distributor action committees. A distributor council is a representative group of distributors selected on the basis of the sizes, structure, and geography that best represent the interests of your entire distribution network.

Distributor councils meet from one to four times a year, and their meetings generate recommendations for the manufacturer on the best ways to handle business issues, such as competitive threats, shared sales support, compensation for national accounts, buying group problems, or channel conflicts.

It is important to keep distributor council meetings on track and not let them digress into a litany of complaints about the manufacturer. To avoid such an unwanted outcome, it is best to rotate membership every few years and rotate the council's leadership. It is important that the distributor council not become a permanent political power base within your distribution channel or organization. It is also important to focus the distributor council on specific issues and defined output relevant to increasing end-user satisfaction.

A distributor action committee is assigned a specific area for manufacturing input, such as assessing distributor training needs, developing a national account policy, or developing an inventory program for parts and service support. Here again, rotate members frequently and have members do pre- and post-workshop assignments to improve the quality and output of each meeting.

A third way to create dialogue is to conduct distributor input sessions at the manufacturer's annual distributor sales conference. Structure the input sessions around relevant topics such as major market trends, competitive threats, and new ideas to improve products. The four keys to more productive distributor input sessions are:

1. predefining subjects,
2. focusing on increasing end-user value,
3. listening to distributor's recommendations without imposing the manufacturer's perspective, and
4. providing participants with the results and actions to be taken.

Committees and input sessions create good will, good communication, new ways to resolve existing problems, and creative ways to increase end-user value.

Reflection Point

How often do we use comprehensive performance evaluations?
▶ Do we conduct product-line performance reviews with all key distributors?
▶ Do we use distributor advisory councils to stimulate strong two-way communication?

Adjustments

The purpose of monitoring is to make appropriate adjustments. There are four levels of adjustments:

1. Level one adjustments are changes of the sales forecast.
2. Level two adjustments are changes to the business plans of the manufacturer or the distributor.
3. Level three adjustments are changing distributors.
4. Level four adjustments are changes of the channel structure.

Sales Forecast Adjustments

Level one adjustments, changes of the sales forecast, are a common and constant part of managing distributor networks. It is normal for a manufacturer to receive monthly sales results from distributors to make rolling forecast corrections. Forecast modifications are then provided to the materials, manufacturing, and inventory management teams as input to their planning activities.

Plan Adjustments

Level two adjustments are changes to manufacturing or distributor business plans. For example; a distributor may add a salesperson, conduct a dealer training event, run a sales incentive program for their sales team, or initiate an on-site inventory program in hopes of increasing a lagging sales performance. A manufacturer may choose to provide the distributor more technical or sales training, increase co-op fund allocation to encourage increased advertising, increase the frequency of RSM visits to provide sales assistance, or provide a direct mail piece to help penetrate a new market segment.

Another option is to change the distributor's strategy to the point of reinventing the distributor's operation plan. An example of reinvention would be creating a specialist department within a generalist distributor. Other systemic adjustments could be made to reduce costs and manage inventory in times of declining sales.

Channel Member Additions or Replacements

Level three adjustments involve the changing of channel members within the existing structure through cancellation, addition, or replacement. If the manufacturer decides the relationship with the distributor is no longer a good fit, it is best for both parties to cancel the contract. Changing distributors is often difficult because distributors do not give up lines easily. A distributor may cease working aggressively to sell a line but not inform the manufacturer. The distributor will hold the line and "milk" it by just taking orders without investing in inventory, credit, promotions, or sales effort.

Distributor atrophy is frustrating to manufacturers. Preventing atrophy requires RSM vigilance and tough action. A distributor cancellation sends a strong message to the other members of the distributor network that the manufacturer will not tolerate lack-luster sales results or effort. Another option being used by manufacturers, because of legal restrictions, is adding a distributor in a struggling territory, thereby creating dual distribution. The most aggressive distributor with the best market fit will prevail; the weak distributor will die out, and the territory will be returned to exclusive distribution as before. Both of these adjustments should take into account the legal and contractual issues discussed in Chapter 4.

Structural Channel Changes

Level four adjustments are structural changes to the channel. Examples of structural changes are selling through sales representatives instead of distributors, using stocking representatives, selling directly to large or national accounts, selling directly to large dealers or buying groups, and establishing new direct sales channels for new immerging market segments.

Although these options may cause increased complexity and conflict with existing channel relationships, they may be the only way to achieve sales coverage in new, shifting, or critical markets. These structural changes were alluded to in the discussion of multiple channels and hybrid channels in Chapter 6. The result of monitoring performance may therefore lead you back to Stage II or III in the channel redesign model, creating in effect a closed loop process. The end becomes a new beginning.

Reflection Point

How well do we make adjustments after monitoring performance?
▶ Do we use all four levels of adjustments?
▶ Are we willing to go through the redesign process when necessary?

Key Points

▶ Monitor distributor sales results monthly to identify major market trends, compare distributor performance, and adjust production schedules.
▶ Monitor distributor activities and changes to gain a "feel" for distributor effectiveness and to obtain early warnings on performance problems.
▶ Make adjustments aggressively. By the time a problem reaches the manufacturer's screen, it requires corrective action.
▶ Build two-way performance evaluation communication into your distributor/manufacturer relationship.

▶ Be prepared to go back to any stage of the channel redesign process to view issues from multiple perspectives as an aid in the change process.

Notes

1. Reviewing other perspectives on measuring channel performance is advisable. Chapter 10 of Louis W. Stern, Adel I. El-Ansary, and Anne Coughlan, *Marketing Channels* (Prentice Hall, 1996), and Chapter 12 of Lawrence G. Friedman and Timothy R. Furey, *The Channel Advantage* (Butterworth Heinemann, 1999), are useful resources.

Index

A

Acquisitions, 10, 33
Action committees, 207–208
Activities, monitoring, 196–197
Activity-based compensation, 16, 95
Adjustments to performance, 208–210
Advertising
  cooperative, 17–18, 128
  planning the use of, 188–193
  by product-line specialists, 169
  as pull strategy, 17
Advocates, 190, 191
Affiliate distributors, 96
Agency for International Development, 106
Agency Sales magazine, 79
Agent Distributor Service, 110
Agents, channel partners as, 102
Aggregation of products, 77
Airtight territories, 57, 96–97
American Association of Exporters & Importers, 107
American National Standards Institute (ANSI), 40
Amway, 32
Ancillary products, 81
Annual distributors' meetings, 149–151, 208
Antitrust laws, 56–60

Application service providers (ASP), 40
Areas of primary responsibility (APRs), 57–58
Assembly, moving closer to end users, 38
Association of Independent Manufacturers'/Representatives, 120
Atrophy of distributors, 209–210
Auditing channels, 85–88
Authorized distributors, 96
Auto malls, 31
Automatic contract renewals, 64
Avon, 4–5

B

Bank of America, 76
Banks
  insurance services, 76
  outsourced functions, 100, 101
Bed liners, 180
Big-box resellers, 5, 137
BIV process, 180
Boise Office Solutions, 82
Branch locations, of potential channel partners, 122
Brightpoint, 75
Broad-line distributors. *See* General line distributors
Brokers, 5–6

Bundling of products, 77
Business functions, shared,
142–143
Business models, changing, 141–142
Business plans
adjusting, 209
of channel partners, 140–141,
151–155
of manufacturers, 140, 149–151
Business strategies, aligning channel strategies with, 23–27
Business-to-business (B2B) channels, 9, 40
Business training, 19. *See also*
Training
Buying behavior, changes with
time, 75
Buying groups, 6
Buying process
decision stage, 181–182
evaluation phase, 179–181
motivation phase, 175–179
relationship stage, 172–175
sales training based on, 170–171

C

Cash flow, importance to distributors, 140
Catalog houses, 6
Category managers, 102
Caterpillar, 94
Change, monitoring, 197–198
Channel Advantage, The, 77
Channel conflicts
changes in nature of, 135
major causes, 95–97
potential for, 12, 83
potential causes, 99
systems to minimize, 94, 99–100
Channel design
international structures,
107–109
international target markets,
105–107

major considerations, 81–83
renovating existing channels,
94–97
Channel effectiveness, 161–162
Channel partners. *See also*
Distributors
business plans, 140–141,
151–155
changing arrangements with,
142–143, 209–210
determining needs of, 30–31
differences from manufacturers,
98–99, 138–141
distributor types, 133–134
evaluating performance, 19,
85–86, 95, 96. *See also*
Performance monitoring
evaluating potential, 123–124
finding, 119–123
forces of change for, 8–10,
135–138, 141–143
influence on channel strategies,
29–30
legal issues with, 55–65
manufacturer's influence with,
134–135
potential, stability of, 122
recruiting, 109–114, 125–129
sales training, 182–188. *See also*
Sales skills training
selling product value to,
163–166
traditional expectations, 148
Channel preferences
data collection, 70–73
designing for, 81–83
major considerations, 74–80
Channel renovation, 94–97
Channel splintering, 33–34
Channels, defined, 5, 6
Circumstances, channel shifting
due to, 74. *See also* Market
changes

Cisco Systems, 94
Closing questions, 178–179
CNH Group, 29
Coaching calls, 175
Coaching product champions
   basic requirements, 168–171
   decision stage skills, 181–182
   evaluation stage skills, 179–181
   motivation stage skills, 175–179
   relationship building skills,
     172–175
   time spent, 167
Collaborative Planning, Forecasting
   and Replenishment (CPFR), 40,
   155
Collaborative strategic alliances,
   42–43
Collusive activity, 56–57
Color impregnation, 38
Commissions, 65
Commodities, 59
Compaq, 46–47
Compatibility of potential channel
   partners, 123
Competence self-evaluation, 93
Competition
   from aftermarket products, 38
   as external influence on channel
     strategies, 34–35
   illegal restraints, 56–57, 59–60
   impact on channel preferences,
     75
Competitive advantage
   demonstrating to channel part-
     ners, 143–144
   differing views of, 139–140
   distribution options for, 11–12
   from environmental conscious-
     ness, 36
Competitors, 84–85, 88
Computer Associates, 15
Computer products
   Dell Inc. channel changes, 4
   hybrid distribution channels, 11

   small business preferences, 4,
     10–11
   value-added resellers, 94
Conservation concerns, 36
Consistency, 93, 144–145
Consolidation of distributors, 10
Consolidators, 137–138
Consultative selling
   questioning skills for, 175–179
   required of distributors, 142
   training for, 193–194
Consumer reps, 6
Contests, 16
Contract labor, 42
Contract manufacturing, 109
Contractors, 137, 176–177
Contracts
   legal terminology, 56–57
   outsourcing, 103
   overview of legal issues, 61–65
Cooperative advertising
   basic features, 17–18
   commitments to channel mem-
     bers, 128
   planning the use of, 188–193
Cost-effectiveness, profitability ver-
   sus, 12
Cost justifications for price differ-
   ences, 60
C-parts consolidators, 137–138
Cross-Cultural Business Behavior,
   113
Cross-cultural differences, 115
Cross Sport bike, 13, 28–29
Culture barriers, 113–114
Cumulative discounts, 16
Customer education, 78
"Customer Insight Reports," 82
Customer preferences
   role in channel strategies,
     10–12, 28–29
   varieties of, 70–73
Customer relationship management
   (CRM), 37

Customer risks, impact on channel fit, 78
Customer stages, 190–192
Customization
customer expectations, 71
impact on channel fit, 77, 81
of promotions for customers, 192–193
Customs service, 106

D

D&H Distributing, 75
Database managers, 39
Data capture technologies, 9, 39
Data coding tools, 39
Data Interchange Standards Association (DISA), 40
Data sources, 106
Dealers. *See also* Channel partners
as competitive advantage for Caterpillar, 94
defined, 6
directories of, 119
exclusive arrangements, 61
training for, 186–188
Deal-focused cultures, 113
Decision-aiding tools, 41
Decision stage of buying process, 181–182
Defenses to antitrust charges, 60
Delivery commitments, 127
Dell Inc., 3–4
Demand forecasting, 41–42
Demand planning, 52
Demographics, 31–32, 74
Demonstration equipment, 129
Department of Agriculture, 106
Department of Commerce, 106
Department of State, 107
Direct channels, 98
Direct customers, 30, 76
Direct exporting, 108
Directories of channel partners, 119–120

Direct sales, 3–4, 5, 94. *See also* E-commerce
Discounts
antitrust issues, 58–60
functional, 164–166
to motivate channel members, 16
Disintermediation, 8, 35
Distance, impact on international channels, 115
Distribution availability, 80
Distributor councils, 207–208
Distributors. *See also* Channel partners
business plans, 140–141, 151–155
directories of, 119
evaluating, 19, 85–86, 95, 96. *See also* Performance monitoring
forces of change for, 8–10, 135–138, 141–143
legal issues with, 55–65
major differences from manufacturers, 138–141
manufacturer's influence with, 134–135
mergers and acquisitions, 33
overview of role, 5
performance profiles, 155–158
recruiting, 125–129
sales training, 182–188
segmenting, 95
selling product value to, 163–166
total number in U.S., 97–98
traditional expectations, 148
treating as partners, 111
types, 133–134
Diversity of customers, 31–32
Drop shipping, 8, 127
Dual distribution, 209–210

E

E-commerce. *See also* Internet
early mistakes, 28

impact on territories, 58, 65
importance of impact on distribution channels, 8–9, 137
as threat to channel members, 99
types of connections for, 39
Economic turbulence, 136
EDI-INT AS2, 9
Electronic Data Interchange for Approved Commercial Transactions (EDIFACT), 40
Electronic monitoring systems, 91–92
Emergency repair parts, 74
Empathy, 93
End-user orientation, 28–29
End-user training, 186
Enterprise Resource Planning (ERP), 40
Enthusiasm, rating distributors on, 157
Environmental concerns, 36
Equipment monitoring systems, 91–92
E-StorePro, 9
European Union (EU), 35
Evaluation. *See also* Measurement, Performance monitoring
distributor enthusiasm, 157
distributor performance, 19, 85–86, 95, 96
distributor potential, 123–124
international channels, 107–109
manufacturers, 87, 88, 158–159
product-line review, 198–208
sales skills training, 185–186, 187
trust levels, 92, 93
Evaluation phase of buying process, 179–181
Evans Industries, 16–17
Evergreen contracts, 63–64
Exclusive dealing, 61
Exclusive territories, 57, 96–97
Exclusivity of product, impact on channel fit, 77

Exel, 51
Existing customer questionnaire, 177–179
Export management companies, 6
Exporting intermediaries, 6, 108
Expressive cultures, 113
Extended warranties, 17

F
Fairness self-evaluation, 93
Federal Trade Commission (FTC) Act, 57
FedEx, 11, 74
Feedback
channel preferences and, 74
for reseller performance assessment, 19
soliciting
from customers, 29
from distributors, 207–208
Film processing, 38
Financial services
changing channel requirements, 76
credit and collections, 100
regulatory changes for, 9–10
First-call questions, 176–177
Fixed-term agreements, 64
Fluid time, 113
Ford Motor Company, 51
Forecasting, 92, 155
Franchisees, 6
Franchising, 109
Functional discounts
basic features, 16
effective use of, 164–166
price differences as, 60

G
Gateway Computers, 11
General line distributors
defined, 6
evaluating, 124
responses to market changes, 136–137

General line distributors (*Cont.*)
strengths and weaknesses, 133–134
Geographic Information Systems (GIS), 40
Geo-spatial Information Technologies (GsIT), 40
Global Positioning Systems (GPS), 40
"Global Study of Supply Chain Leadership and Its Impact on Business Performance, A," 45–46
Globalization, 92
Goals. *See also* Strategy
aligning with resellers, 15
basing sales training on, 183
channel design and, 91–92
in distributor business plans, 140–141, 152
Goodyear, 51
Government Export Portal, 107
Government regulations. *See* Regulations
Gramm-Leach-Bliley Act, 9–10
Grange Mutual Insurance, 76
Gray markets, 115–116
Grocery chains, 101
Gross margin return on inventory investment (GMROI), 84, 141
Growability of distributors, 86
Guarantees, 17

H

Harley-Davidson, 180
Healthcare industry, 49, 91–92
Heating, ventilation, and air conditioning industry, 137
Hewlett-Packard, 46–47
High-importance products, 126
High-touch channels, 76–78, 81
Hispanic-American population trends, 31–32
Home Depot, 100, 124
Honeywell, 9

Horizontal restraints, 56
Hospitals, 49
House accounts, 98–99
Huffy, 13, 28–29
Human resources management policies, 42
Hybrid channels
building, 100–103
defined, 5, 6
evaluating potential partners for, 124
examples, 11

I

IBM, 94
Ideal candidate template, 120, 121
Incentives, 186. *See also* Motivation
Independent reps
contracts for, 65
defined, 5, 6
directories of, 119–120
Indirect channels, 76–77, 98
Indirect exporting, 108
Indirect materials, 34
Indirect sales, 5
Industrial reps, 6
Industries, impact on channel preferences, 76
Influencers, 7
Informal managers, 113
Information technologies
hypothetical market segment preferences, 71–73
as internal influence on channel strategies, 39–41
outsourced functions, 101–102
Ingram Micro, 8
Innovation, 46
Instant Messaging (IM), 32
Insurance agencies, 10
Integrators, 7
Integrity self-evaluation, 93
Intelligent Character Recognition (ICR), 40

Interdependence self-evaluation, 93
Intermediaries, 7
International channels
    evaluating designs, 107–109
    managing, 115–116
    structures in, 107–109
    target markets, 105–107
International Monetary Fund, 107
*International Trade Statistics
    Yearbook*, 107
Internet. *See also* E-commerce
    early mistakes, 28
    importance of impact on distri-
        bution channels, 8–9
    as information technology
        option, 39–41
    as international marketing tool,
        110
    splintering of channels by, 33–34
    as threat to channel members,
        99
Inventory, price protection for, 127
Inventory management
    impact of Internet on, 9
    improving with supply chain
        management, 48–49
    by product-line specialists, 169
    recent trends, 142–143
    sales calls for, 173
Inventory training, 19

J
JC Penney, 4–5, 49–50
Jobbers, 7
Just-in-time inventory, 75

K
Key accounts, 170
Key result areas, 27
Knowledge self-evaluation, 93

L
Labeling process, 38–39
Labor force trends, 32, 42
Lands' End, 10, 26

Large customers' needs, 82
Lead-by-example calls, 175
Lead generation, 124, 128
Leasing dealers, 142
Levi Strauss & Company, 99–100
Licensing, 109
Listening skills, 179
Literature update calls, 173
Logistics services, 42, 101, 102–103
Logistics strategies, 53
Long-term contracts, 16
Low-touch channels, 76–78, 81
Loyalty segments, 190–192
Lynch, Robert Porter, 46

M
Maintenance calls, 172–174
Major products
    defined, 126, 135
    training for, 128
Management issues, 14–15, 97–100
Management reporting tools, 40
Management styles, 113
Manitowoc Ice Machines, 142, 144
Manufacturers
    business plans, 140, 149–151
    changing distributor relation-
        ships, 142–143, 209–210
    distributor conflicts with, 98–99
    distributors' assessment, 87, 88,
        158–159
    influence over distributors,
        134–135
    major differences from distribu-
        tors, 138–141
    traditional expectations, 148
Manufacturers' Agents National
    Association (MANA), 79, 119
Manufacturers' Representatives
    Educational Research
    Foundation, 119–120
Manufacturers' reps, 5, 119–120
Manufacturing processes, 38–39,
    76

Manufacturing strategies, 52–53
Market changes, 8–10, 135–138
Market channel grids, 73
Market coverage, 79–83
Market penetration, 159–160
Market planning, 169
Market potential, 79–80, 105–106
Marketing
    channels defined, 5
    distributor training, 19
    legal issues, 57–61
    to potential channel partners,
      125–129
Mass retailers, 13, 28–29
Master distributors, 7
Maturity of products, 78
Maximum prices, 58
Measurement. *See also* Evaluation
    channel effectiveness, 84–85
    of channel partner performance,
      19, 85–86, 95, 96
    in distributor business plans, 152
    enterprise performance score-
      cards, 42
    market potential, 79–80
    performance monitoring meth-
      ods, 195–198
    product-line reviews, 198–208
    product-line specialist duties, 170
    supply chain effectiveness, 47
Medical equipment monitoring sys-
    tems, 91–92
Mergers and acquisitions, 10, 33
Metrics. *See* Measurement
Micro pilot analyses, 50–52
Microsoft, 94, 95
Mid-interview questions, 178
Minimum prices, 58
Minor products, 126, 135
Missed opportunity calls, 173
Mission statements, 26
Modular product design, 41
Monitoring channel performance,
    85–88, 152–153

Motivation
    in buying process, 175–179
    of channel members, 16–17, 164
    for sales training, 186
MRO distributors, 7
Multiple channels, managing,
    97–100

N

National Association of
    Manufacturers, 106
National Association of Wholesale
    Distributors, 119
National Trade Data Bank, 107
Nationwide Financial Services,
    9–10
Navarre Distribution Services, 75
Negotiations, 65, 78
New business development calls,
    174, 176–177
New Holland tractors, 29
New product launches, 12–14, 37
Nike, 12
Nongrowables, 86
"No returns" programs, 82
North American Industry
    Classification System, 159
North Scottsdale Auto Mall, 31

O

Observation, 29
Off-the-shelf products, 76, 81
Online marketing. *See* E-commerce;
    Internet
Opening questions, 177–178
Operational capabilities, 122–123,
    157
Operations scheduling, 41–42
Operations strategies, 52–53
Optical Character Recognition
    (OCR), 40
Ordering systems, 9
Outsourcing
    defined, 7
    in hybrid channels, 100–103

impact on channel preferences, 76

as internal influence on channel strategies, 41–42

Owens Corning, 99

P

Packaging operations, 38–39

Parker Hannifin, 137

Partners. *See* Channel partners

Partnership relationship management, 95

Pass-through material, 18

Payment terms, 128

Penda Corporation, 180

Penetration indexes, 159–160, 196

Performance measurement. *See* Evaluation; Measurement

Performance monitoring

basic methods, 195–198

making adjustments, 208–210

product-line review, 198–208

Performance standards

in contracts, 62, 63, 64

distributor plans, 151–155

distributor profiles, 155–158

establishing, 83–84

evaluating manufacturers, 158–159

manufacturer plans, 149–151

penetration indexes, 159–160, 196

traditional expectations, 147–149

Physical distribution, 7

Pilot projects, 50–52

Planning. *See* Business plans

Point-of-installation technologies, 9

Point-of-sale technologies, 9

Policies of partner customers, 30

Population trends, 31–32

Positioning price, 180–181

Practical availability of discounts, 60

Predatory pricing, 59

Premier distributors, 95–96

Pricing

legal issues, 57, 58–60

presenting in sales call, 180–181

protecting distributors from changes, 127

Primary line competition, 59

Primary products, 126

Prioritizing, 27

Prizes, 16–17

Problems, soliciting customer feedback about, 74

Product availability expectations, 71

Product champions. *See also* Coaching product champions

importance, 162

responsibilities, 168, 169–170

selecting, 166–168

Product Distribution Law Guide, The, 55

Product fit, 80, 121

Product importance to potential channel partners, 125–127

Product life cycles

aligning channel strategies with, 13–14, 37–38

impact on channel fit, 78, 124

Product-line fit, 121

Product-line performance reviews, 198–208

Product-line specialists. *See* Product champions

Product requirements, 76–79

Product training, 18, 182–188

Profit pass-over policies, 58

Profitability, cost-effectiveness versus, 12

Program review calls, 174

Promotional reserve funds, 188–190

Promotional support

basic features, 17–18

commitments to channel members, 128

planning the use of, 188–193

Prospects, 190, 191
Pull strategies, 17, 145
Push strategies, 17–18, 145

Q
Questioning skills, 175–179
Quick wins (supply chain management), 50–52

R
Radio frequency data collection (RFDC), 40
Radio frequency identification (RFID) tags, 9, 40
Rapid delivery commitments, 127
Recycling, 39
Redesign phases, 20–21
Referrals, finding channel partners through, 119
Regional sales managers. *See also* Sales skills training
    major responsibilities, 163–164
    monitoring distributor activities, 196–198
    product champion selection and coaching, 166–171
Regional warehousing, 128
Regulations
    as external influence on channel strategies, 35–36
    impact on distribution channels, 9–10
    terminology, 56–57
Reintermediation, 41–42
Relationship building, 172–175
Relationship-focused cultures, 113
Remote monitoring systems, 91–92
Reputation of potential channel partners, 123
Resale motivations, 164
Resellers, 7, 14–19. *See also* Channel partners; Distributors
Reserved cultures, 113–114
Respect self-evaluation, 93
Restraints of trade, 56–57

Retailing, 49–50, 75
Return on investment (ROI), 50–52
Rheem Manufacturing, 137
Ride-along sales support, 128
Rigid time, 113
Risk
    to customers, 78
    to distributors, 140
Robinson-Patman Act, 57, 58–60
Rule of reason, 56–57

S
Sales
    changing for distributors, 142
    channel partner capabilities, 122
    differing views of, 138–139
    forecasting, 52, 208–209
    monitoring distributor activities, 195–197
    translating strategies into calls, 145
Sales plans, 163, 165
Sales promotions, 16
Sales skills training
    as basic partnership benefit, 18
    coaching overview, 168–171
    consultative selling, 193–194
    decision stage strategies, 181–182
    for distributor salespeople, 182–188
    evaluation phase strategies, 179–181
    motivation phase strategies, 175–179
    relationship building strategies, 172–175
Sales support programs, 18, 128
Scheduling sales training, 183
Sears, 10, 26
Secondary line competition, 60
Secondary products, 126, 135
Segmentation
    of markets, 32, 71–73
    of partner customers, 30–31, 95

Selection criteria, international channel partners, 112, 113
Self-growing distributors, 86
Services of potential channel partners, 123
Shared calls, 175
Sherman Act, 56–57
Short-term planning, 152
Simplicity of plans and strategies, 143, 152
Situation analysis, 24
SkidResistor, 180
Small contractors, 137
Specialized channels, 14, 124
Specialty distributors
    defined, 7
    evaluating, 124
    responses to market changes, 136
    strengths and weaknesses, 134
Specifiers, 7
Spiffs, 17
Splintering of traditional channels, 33–34
Stability of potential channel partners, 122
Standard closing questions, 178–179
Standard contracts, 61–62
Standard Industrial Classification (SIC) code, 159
Standard opening questions, 177–178
Staples, 82
State Farm Insurance, 76
Stock rotation programs, 128
Stocking resellers, 7
Strategic fit
    effect of market dynamics on, 8–10
    overview, 3–8
    product life cycle and, 12–14
    strategy changes and, 10–12
Strategic sourcing, 52

Strategy
    assessing ability to implement, 143–145
    channel versus business, 23–27
    external influences, 28–36
    internal forces, 36–44
    maintaining control, 111
    shifts in, 10–12
Structural channel changes, 210
Substitution, 78
Success story calls, 173
Supplier relationship management (SRM), 37
Suppliers. *See* Manufacturers
Supply Chain Council, 52
Supply chain management
    business case for, 48–50
    core processes, 52–53
    as internal influence on channel strategies, 43–44
    meeting reseller needs, 45–47
    quick wins, 50–52
Supply Chain Value-Added Networks, 40
Supply chains, defined, 7
Support programs. *See also* Sales skills training
    customer expectations, 71
    overview, 17–19, 86
    promotional, 17–18, 128, 188–193
    technical, 18, 71, 157
Surgical supply dealers, 33
Surveys, 29, 87, 88
Suspects, 190, 191
Synthetic channels, 6
Synthetic products, 38
System integrators, 7

T
TAL Apparel Ltd., 49–50
Target markets, 140, 190–192
Team relationships, 37
Team Value Management (TVM), 51

Technical support programs
  customer expectations, 71
  to motivate channel members, 18
  rating distributors on, 157
Templates
  channel partner value assessment, 96
  distributor profiles, 156
  ideal channel member candidate, 120, 121
  product-line reviews, 199–206
  sales skills training evaluation, 187
  trust assessment, 93
Termination of contracts, 62, 63
Terms of sale, 64
Territories
  determining extent of coverage, 79–80
  exclusive, 57, 96–97
  legal issues, 57–58, 63, 64
  of potential channel partners, 121–122
Third-party intermediaries, as agents, 102
Time frames
  for contracts, 63–64
  cultural differences, 113
  manufacturer's versus distributor's, 140–141
Tissue paper manufacturers, 47, 48
TLC, Inc., 101
Total solutions, customer expectations for, 71
Trade missions, 110
Trading areas, gauging market potential, 79
Training. *See also* Sales skills training
  to motivate channel members, 18–19
  for potential channel members, 128
  by product-line specialists, 169

  for product-line specialists, 170–171
  promoting to distributors, 174
Trane Company, 100, 143
Translation of strategies into sales calls, 145
Trust levels, 92, 93, 123
Two-way communication self-evaluation, 93
Tying arrangements, 61

U
United Nations, 107
U.S. Agency for International Development, 106
U.S. Census, 79
U.S. Customs Service, 106
U.S. Department of Agriculture, 106
U.S. Department of Commerce, 106
U.S. Department of State, 107
U.S. Government Export Portal, 107

V
Value-added resellers, 7, 94
Value chains, defined, 7
Vertical integration, 8
Vertical restraints, 56
Vision, 26–27, 78–79
Vision statements, 26
Volume discounts, 16, 95
Volvo GM Heavy Truck Corporation, 11, 74

W
Wal-Mart, 9
Warehousing, 128
Warranties, 17, 127
Web sites
  Agency for International Development, 106
  American Association of Exporters & Importers, 107
  Association of Independent Manufacturers'/Representatives, 120
  Customs Service, 106

Data Interchange Standards
Association, 40
Department of Agriculture, 106
Department of Commerce, 106
Department of State, 107
Government Export Portal, 107
International Monetary Fund, 107
*International Trade Statistics
Yearbook*, 107
Manufacturers' Agents National
Association, 119
Manufacturers' Representatives
Educational Research
Foundation, 119
manufacturers' use of, 9, 137
National Association of
Manufacturers, 106
National Association of
Wholesale Distributors, 119
National Trade Data Bank, 107
United Nations, 107
U.S. Agency for International
Development, 106

U.S. Census, 79
U.S. Customs Service, 106
U.S. Department of Agriculture,
106
U.S. Department of Commerce,
106
U.S. Department of State, 107
U.S. Government Export Portal,
107
World Bank, 106
World Trade Centers Association,
106
"White-box PCs," 4
Wholesale drop shipping, 8
Wholesalers, 5, 8. *See also* Channel
partners
Win rates, 80
World Bank, 106
World Trade Centers Association,
106
Written contracts. *See* Contracts
W. W. Grainger, 33, 134

About the Authors

All three authors are on the Executive Education faculty of the UW-Madison School of Business.

Linda Gorchels is the director of marketing seminars and has been offering executive education programs on marketing through distributors for more than a decade. She has provided training and consulting on a wide range of marketing topics and is the author of *The Product Manager's Handbook* and *The Product Manager's Field Guide*. Prior to joining the university she held marketing management, marketing research, product management/development, and acquisitions positions with VEREX Assurance, Wm. C. Brown Publishers, and Lear-Siegler, Inc.

Ed Marien is the director of supply chain, procurement, and transportation management seminars, offering educational programs for industry practitioners from manufacturers, distributors, and third-party providers. Ed has been employed directly in and consults extensively with industry executives on supply chain economics and business planning. He is very active with professional and trade associations, having held many national and chapter positions. He has authored many journal and trade magazine articles and is often quoted on issues of national interest.

Chuck West is the director of sales seminars for UW-Executive Education, as well as for the *Center for the Advanced Studies in Business, Inc.* His prior experience includes running his own consulting firm for 20 years, working in market management, sales management, sales, and marketing research capacities for 3M, working as a management scientist at Honeywell, and being involved in sales and market analysis for the Ford Motor Company. He holds the top rating on the national speakers lists of the American Marketing Association and Sales & Marketing Executives.